Other works by Carl Reiner:

Enter Laughing

The 2000 Year Old Man:
The Complete History

All Kinds of Love

Continue Laughing

The 2000 Year Old Man in
the Year 2000: The Book

How Paul Robeson Saved My Life
And Other Mostly Happy Stories

My Anecdotal Life

NNNNN

Just Desserts: A Novellelah

I Remember Me

I Just Remembered

Children's books by Carl Reiner:

Tell Me A Scary Story
But Not Too Scary!

The 2000 Year Old Man
Goes To School

Tell Me Another Scary Story
But Not Too Scary!

Tell Me A Silly Story

Too Scared To Scream

The Secret Treasure Of Kahka Paka

WHAT I FORGOT TO REMEMBER

CARL REINER

RANDOM™
CONTENT
PUBLISHING

RANDOM CONTENT™
Beverly Hills, CA 90210
www.RandomContent.com

Published by RANDOM CONTENT 03/20/15

ISBN: 978-0-9915368-1-8

Front cover painting by Estelle Reiner
Back cover photo by Unknown

Design by Aaron Davis

Any people depicted in images have given approval by their estate and trustees.

This book is printed on acid-free paper.

Because of the dynamic nature of the Internet, any web addresses or links contained in this book may have changed since publication and may no longer be valid.

Doris Day, James Garner and my first screenplay "The Thrill Of It All"

Me as "the fool in charge" directing Victoria Tennant & Steve Martin
during filming of "All Of Me"

"Inviting people to laugh at you when you are laughing at yourself is a good thing to do. You may be the fool but you're the fool in charge."

Carl Reiner – "My Anecdotal Life*"
– "I Remember Me*"
– "I Just Remembered*"

Contents

Me as Gen. Von Kluk in "Dead Men Don't Wear Plaid"

REAL TIME
WITH
BILL MAHER

Foreword

Carl Reiner keeps remembering, and we are the beneficiaries. What a life! And what memories: stories about Sinatra and Billy Holiday, Tyrone Power and Peter Seeger, the Rosenbergs and Milton Berle – and, of course, family – Estelle Reiner, Rob Reiner, Mel Brooks…

Let me take a moment to offer a remembrance of my own. In 1989 I was finishing up the decade where I tried to be an actor and make it big in sitcoms. Having starred in "Sara" "Hard Knocks" and "Charlie Hoover" (don't worry, nobody else does either), the fledgling Fox Network was ready to give young Bill his own sitcom, created by Garry Shandling and myself. It was called "Bill Gets A Life," and I wanted it to be my generation's "Dick Van Dyke Show."

As a kid, that was one show that I never outgrew – that, in fact, as I got older and kept watching reruns, I appreciated more and more. Worshiped may be the more accurate word. And for good reason: It was, and remains, the most sophisticated half hour comedy ever on television that is also flat out LOL. Not that we knew what LOL meant in the 60s.

If you remember the show where Danny Thomas played an alien and Rob lost his thumbs, then you remember the classic "Walnut" show. So does its creator, and to read the backstory within these pages was worth the price of admission alone. Well, I read it for free in galleys, I don't know how much you paid. But if I may be so bold, Carl: how about for your next book, the story of every episode of the Van Dyke show?

I'll be waiting.

Oh, and "Bill Gets A Life"? Still waiting for that pickup, Fox!

-Bill Maher

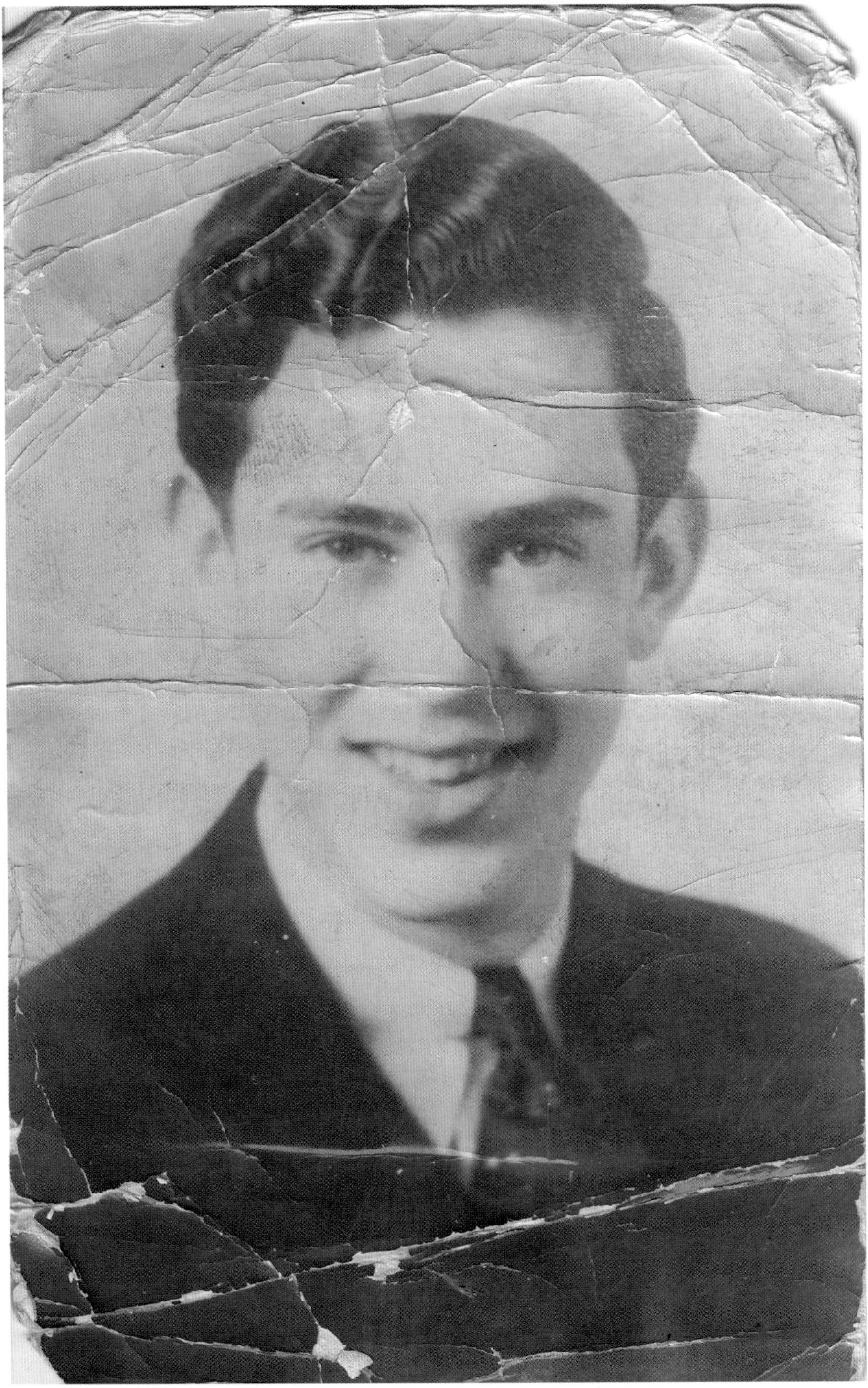

Me at 16 graduating from Evander Childs High School, Bronx, New York – 1938

Preface

I had no intention of writing a third memoir after writing "I Remember Me" and "I Just Remembered," but when remembering some of the things I forgot to remember, "What I Forgot To Remember" was born.

–Carl Reiner 2015

For Rob, Annie & Lucas

Finding the Proper Resting Place for a Beloved's Cheap Ukulele

CHAPTER ONE

Finding the Proper Resting Place for a Beloved's Cheap Ukulele

Many years before I ever met Estelle Lebost, the lovely person who, for reasons no one including myself will ever comprehend, agreed to become my wife, she was considered by her family and friends to be a whiz at strumming a ukulele. Serious musicians never considered the four-stringed ukulele to be a legitimate instrument and ranked it just ahead of the kazoo and miles behind its closest relative, the six-string guitar. In the twenties and thirties the world deigned to accept and even admire Cliff Edwards, a virtuoso of the benighted instrument.

Cliff Edwards, who was dubbed "Ukulele Ike" recorded many of his songs which are currently available on the internet. Among these classics are:

"Somebody Loves Me"

"It Had to Be You"

"I'll See You In My Dreams"

"Melancholy Baby"

"Love Is Just Around The Corner" and the little known,

"My Old Girl Is My New Girl Now"

Authur Godfrey

In the late 1940's and early 50's the Ukulele had a new champion, Arthur Godfrey. On his daily TV show he tickled his audiences by singing a few ditties while accompanying himself on his Uke.

In the 1960's, a tall, gawky, left handed entertainer who billed himself as "Tiny Tim" brought the ukulele back into the spotlight. This straggle-haired performer was a frequent guest on both Johnny Carson's

Tiny Tim

"The Tonight Show" and "Rowan and Martin's Laugh In." His recording of, "Tiptoe Through The Tulips," made Billboard's list of top twenty hits and it sold over 200,000 copies. Tiny Tim went on to give sold-out performances in Las Vegas and in concert halls throughout the nation.

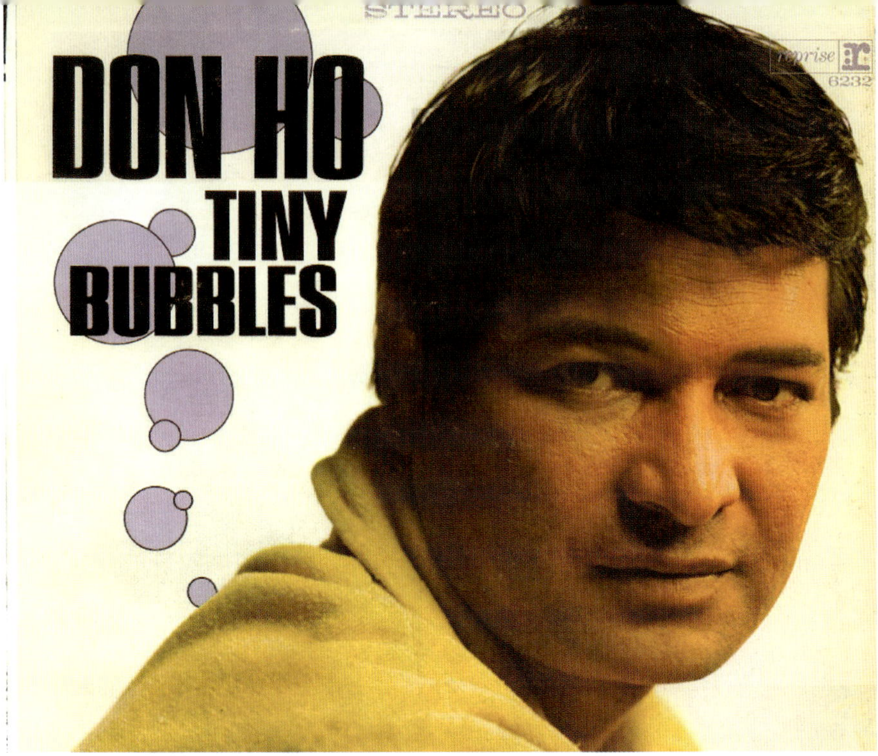

Don Ho

Don Ho, Hawaii's gifted and popular troubadour did much to keep the Ukulele in a spotlight.

Thinking about Don Ho and his signature song, "Tiny Bubbles," brought another Hawaiian ditty to mind. It dealt with papayas and an island Princess named Papuli. I wondered if this song was listed anywhere, and by gum, it was! By Googling it, I learned that the song was written and sung by Harry Owens and its alliterative title was:

"PRINCESS POO-POO-LY HAS PLENTY PA-PA-YAS"

There were a few verses, and the last one ended with the following double entendre lyrics:

"Princess Pupuli has plenty papayas,
She loves to give them away
And all the neighbors they say
She may give you the fruit but she holds on to the root
And she has both the fruit and the root to boot
Zazza zazza zsazza zazza zay."

Eddie Vedder

In recent times the most prestigious practitioner of the ukulele is the popular lead singer of "Pearl Jam," Eddie Vedder.

And now to explain why I titled this chapter "Finding The Proper Resting Place For A Beloved's Cheap Ukulele." In an earlier memoir, I had written how my wife, the former Estelle Lebost, when she was a wee lass of thirteen, sat on a blanket at Orchard Beach and entertained her friends by singing and playing her uke. I wrote about how a perceptive radio producer happened by and asked if she would like to sing her songs on WBNX, a Bronx radio station. She said she would, and for three consecutive Saturday afternoons Estelle, accompanying herself on the ukulele, sang and played. She was so well received by the listeners that the producer offered her a weekly gig, which she had to decline.

" I'm about to start high school," she explained, "and even if I weren't, I couldn't take the job because those songs are the only ones I know."

In my bio, "I Remember Me," I wrote extensively of Estelle's myriad of talents as an artist, a jazz singer, a wife, a mother and a dedicated political activist, but I did not underline the amount of fun our family and friends had because Estelle, who had a 'Venus Fly Trap' ear for music, could play and sing hundreds of popular songs. Some were current and some from 'the days of yore.' If you could hum it, she could play it. Estelle could not read music, but because of her ear, was able to play the correct chords needed for our sing-alongs.

I am so pleased that I encouraged her to record the two albums that feature her singing and strumming her ukulele, albums that are aptly titled, "Ukulele Mama" and "Ukulele Mama 2," this led to her recording more ukulele featured albums, including, "Grown Up Songs For Kids," which, I daresay, was a true labor of love.

Estelle felt sad when she contemplated children growing up today and having no knowledge of or access to the songs of the nineteen twenties and thirties.

To give the 'young-uns' an opportunity to hear these treasured songs, she chose 27 of her favorites and had them arranged and orchestrated to accommodate the ability of young children to hear and understand the lyrics. Hoping that boys and girls would sing along with her, Estelle sang at a slow tempo and clearly enunciated the lyrics.

And what do you know? It worked! Many friends reported that their tots, who ordinarily, when strapped in a car seat, were prone to be fidgety, would sit calmly and smile when they heard Estelle's voice singing songs like **"A You're Adorable," "I, Yi, Yi, Yi, I Like You Very Much,"** and **"Show Fly Pie!"**

I have loaded all of Estelle's seven Jazz CDs into my car radio and when driving, by listening to a few of the 137 songs she recorded, I once again have the pleasure of her company.

Now, how I came to title this piece, "Finding The Proper Resting Place For A Beloved's Cheap Ukulele:"

In a back bedroom of my home, which is now used as a catch-all for items that are too good to throw out, I found the original, inexpensive ukulele Estelle had used at the "Gardenia" when, at my prodding, she first added a few classic ukulele accompanied songs to her regular program of Jazz and Blues. I felt strongly that she deserved to have a finer instrument than the cheap one she had and to that end we visited an old established guitar shop on Sunset Boulevard.

The store was a major purveyor of the esteemed Martin Guitar and the sales person was surprised to learn that we were looking for a ukulele. He smiled and asked us to follow him into a large room full of guitars, where he trotted out a beautifully crafted uke that was made by The Martin Guitar Company.

Estelle balked when she heard its price, but after strumming it and hearing its mellow tone, I was able to convince her that she deserved to own a Martin–and that we could afford it.

Now, as I looked sadly at the old, cheap ukulele, I realized that I had not paid proper attention to the instrument my dear wife had once owned and played. It deserved a better resting place than a cluttered shelf.

After Estelle's passing, I had decided to keep our master bedroom as it was when she last slept there.

When preparing to perform at the Gardenia, she rehearsed in that bedroom where she kept her standing microphone, reel-to-reel recorder, and amplifier. The wooden stool she used when playing her uke at the club now stands at the fireplace and atop the stool sits a brown paper-wrapped corrugated box that contains her ashes.

In her last year, while in bed, hoping to recover from her illness, Estelle kept a list of songs from which she would choose the ones to sing for her monthly gigs at the Gardenia Supper Club.

'*What better place,*' I thought, '*for her old uke to be, but on this bed.*'

In 2008, before she passed, she had given her sturdy Martin ukulele to our son Lucas, whose studio I visited recently to see his new oil paintings. There I, and a discerning and appreciative crowd, viewed his fifteen brilliantly wrought colorful works on large canvases.

After being served drinks and petits fours, Luke picked up his Mom's uke, and led the happy crowd in a community sing-along, of great oldies, which included many of his Mom's favorites. He ending the evening with a touching rendition of...

"Bye Bye Blackbird"

Pack up all my cares and woes
Feeling low here I go
Bye bye blackbird

Where somebody waits for me
Sugar sweet so is she
Bye bye blackbird

No one seems to love or understand me
And all the hard luck stories they keep handing me
Where somebody shines the light
I'll be coming on home tonight
Bye bye blackbird

Nobody seems to love or understand me
And all the hard luck stories they keep on handing me
Where somebody shines the light
I'm coming on home tonight
Blackbird, Bye Bye!
Blaaaaaack Biiiiirrrd Byeeeee, Bye!"

Lucas Reiner

Frankie Sang It Better But I Sang It First

Abel Meeropol aka Lewis Allan

CHAPTER TWO

Frankie Sang It Better But I Sang It First

In 1942, Frank Sinatra, who in later years was dubbed "The Voice," recorded a song that, a year earlier I had introduced at Allaben Acres, an adult summer resort nestled in New York's picturesque Adirondack Mountains.

There are three more names that truly belong in the title but I thought that adding the names, Lewis Allan, Anne Saxe and Vivian Rifkin, would make it too cumbersome-- and cumbersomeness is something I have always assiduously tried to avoid. I should have probably avoided using the words 'cumbersomeness' and 'assiduously'-- I just might delete them before this goes to press--we'll see.

For eight weeks that summer at Allaben Acres, the politically left-of-center rustic resort, Lewis Allan was the entertainment staff's resident songwriter. For ten months of the year, Lewis Allan was gainfully employed as an English teacher at DeWitt Clinton High School, where his Bronx students knew him as Mr. Abel Meeropol, his birth name.

It was in the summer of '42 I had the good fortune to be asked to take part in an evening of classical music and sing a song Lewis Allan had written. It was the brilliant concert pianist, Vivian Rifkin, who had chosen me to be the lead singer in a performance of "The House I Live In."

The gifted Miss Rifkin, who gave solo recitals at Carnegie and Town Hall, helped me to overcome my fear of singing off key and out of rhythm, something for which I was famous.

Vivian actually succeeded in coaching me to sing well enough to keep me smiling about it for almost 72 years. Often as I go on my morning stroll, I find myself singing the poetically patriotic lyrics of "The House I Live In," which are:

The House I Live In

Lyrics by Lewis Allan & Music by Earl Robinson

"What is America to me? A name, a map, the flag I see,
A certain word "Democracy." What is America to me?

The house I live in, the friends that I have found,
The folks behind the railroad and the people all around,
The worker and the farmer, and the sailor on the sea,
The men who built this country, that's America to me.

The house I live in, the neighbors white and black,
The people who just came here, or from generations back,
The Town Hall and the soap box, the torch of liberty,
A place to speak my mind out, that's America to me.

The house I live in, the goodness everywhere,
A land of wealth and beauty and with enough for all to share,
A house that we call freedom, the home of Liberty,
and the promise of tomorrow, that's America to me.

The town I live in, the street, the house, the room,
The pavement of the city or a garden all in bloom,
The church, the school, the clubhouse, a million lights to see,
But especially the people, that's America to me.

Not long after I introduced "The House I Live In" lyrics by Abel Meerapol and music by George Kliensinger), it was sung and recorded by many of my 'fellow artists,' they being:

Mahalia Jackson, Paul Robeson, Josh White, Sonny Rollins, The Ravens, Tony Danza-- AND The Chairman of the Board, Frank Sinatra! Besides recording "The House I Live In," he also starred in an Academy Award winning short film featuring the song.

I freely admit that Frankie and those other great artists sang "The House I Live In" as it deserved to be sung!

Note: In a 2003 bio, "My Anecdotal Life," I wrote of other fascinating folk I had encountered at Allaben in the summer of '42. Among those were: Bernie Hern, my comedy mentor, Paul Petroff, a creative production designer, his assistant, Stella Lebost and Maestro Sidney Bechet, the brilliant soprano saxophonist and Jazz icon.

Sidney Bechet followed in the footsteps of the great trumpet virtuoso, Joe "King" Oliver and his protégé, Louis Armstrong. Those men, along with pianist Jelly Roll Morton and composer Scott Joplin ,were the pioneers of American music! Ragtime, Jazz and Dixieland was their gift to the world.

Sidney Bechet

Joe "King" Oliver

Louis Armstrong

Jelly Roll Morton

Scott Joplin

Stella Lebost

Audra McDonald, Billie Holiday, Stella Lebost & "Strange Fruit"

CHAPTER THREE

Audra McDonald, Billie Holiday, Stella Lebost & "Strange Fruit"

I first learned of Billie Holiday in the summer of 1942 from my then girlfriend, Stella. Billie Holiday, often billed as 'Lady Day,' was one of the truly great interpreters of Blues and Jazz and only Ella Fitzgerald, Carmen McRae and Anita O'Day belonged in that vaunted circle. I believe that Stella (my then future wife) would have added Audra McDonald's name to her list had she seen her performance on Broadway where she successfully channels Billie Holiday, a performance for which Audra MacDonald received her sixth Tony Award.

It was the summer of '42 when I first heard a song that Billie Holiday had recorded in 1939. The melody was haunting and the lyrics were considered to be controversial and inflammatory, as they dealt with the deep south and its pernicious racism. The music and lyrics were written by Lewis Allan and in 1999, Time Magazine voted it the song of the century–it was titled "Strange Fruit."

In her signature liquid style, Billie Holiday sang:

Strange Fruit

Lyrics & Music by Lewis Allan

Southern trees bear a strange fruit,
Blood on the leaves and blood at the root,
Black body swinging in the Southern breeze,
Strange fruit hanging from the Poplar trees.

Pastoral scene of the gallant South,
The bulging eyes and the twisted mouth,
Scent of Magnolia sweet and fresh,
And the sudden smell of burning flesh!

Here is a fruit for the crows to pluck,
For the rain to gather, for the wind to suck,
For the sun to rot, for a tree to drop,
Here is a strange and bitter crop.

Billie Holiday

Abel Meerapol and his wife Anne chose 'Lewis Allan' as his pen name to honor their two infant boys Lewis and Allan who had died at birth.

In 1953, Abel Meerapol, ever the champion of the downtrodden, became aware of the plight of two young orphan boys, ten year old Michael and six year old Robert, whose parents Julius and Ethel Rosenberg had been tried and convicted as being spies for the Soviet Union. The Rosenbergs were the first United States citizens to be put to death in peace time.

Julius Rosenberg

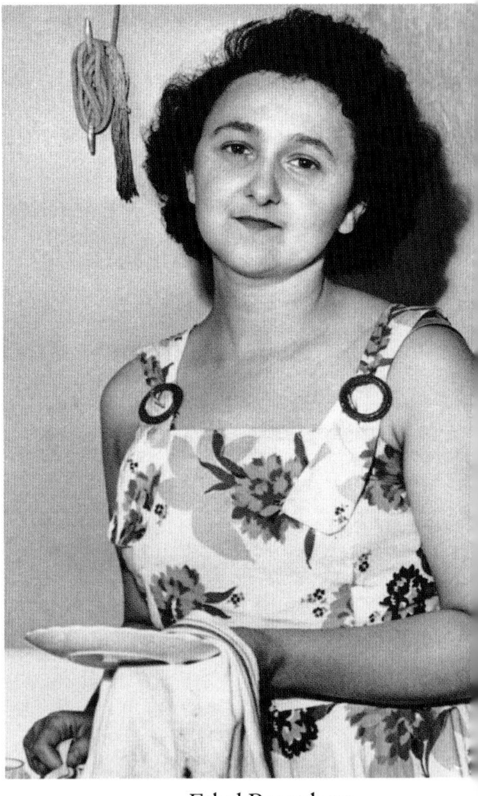

Ethel Rosenberg

Hundreds of newspaper columns and dozens of books have been written about the trial and the Rosenbergs' steadfast claim of being innocent. The most damaging witness was Ethel's brother, David Greenglass, who later admitted that he had perjured himself when he lied about his sister and her husband's involvement in espionage.

David Greenglass

Robert & Michael Rosenberg

The newspapers featured stories about the plight of the two orphaned Rosenberg children who, having no relatives willing to risk adopting them, were now wards of the state. Abel Meerapol and his wife Anne Saxe filed adoption papers and were granted custody of the boys.

Abel felt strongly that if their adopted sons retained their surname, Rosenberg, a permanent stigma would forever follow them. He suggested they take his name and be Michael and Robert Meerapol.

With loving care, guided by their stepparents, the children grew up to be outstanding citizens.

Today Michael and Richard Meerapol are directors of "The Rosenberg Fund For Children," an organization that does for the poor and the needy what Abel and Anne did for them. Every year, I am happy to be able to contribute to the brothers Meerapol's most worthwhile organization.

Robert Meeropol

Michael Meeropol

?

The Improvenator: The Ultimate Appliance

Irving Reiner & Son

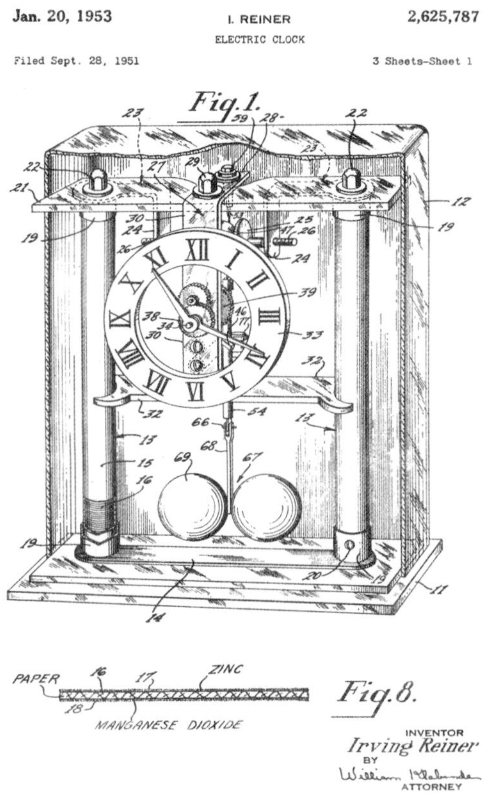

Irving Reiner's US Patent for battery powered clock

CHAPTER FOUR

The Improvenator: The Ultimate Appliance

Until recently, the genes with which my father gifted me ninety-three years ago had been lying dormant. Irving Reiner was an inventor and was granted U.S. patents for his invention of the battery powered clock and for a dry-pile battery which had a shelf life of one hundred years. I do feel that I can credit his creative genes for infusing me with the ability to think up ideas that spawned the writing of novels, television shows and films, but this year, for the first time, I had an idea that led me to create something tangible, something with working parts like the cotton gin or the combustible engine—a real product! I dubbed my new product "The Improvenator."

To build "The Improvenator" I used real tools, tools like a hammer, a chisel, screwdrivers, a skill saw and a metal shaping lathe that I rented for three months.

I choose not to burden you with the details but I will say that building the "The Improvenator" was a tedious, time consuming effort and, oft times, a frustrating one. I had decided not to elicit the aid or advice of professional electricians, carpenters or blueprint makers, knowing that a discouraging word from an expert might give me second thoughts about continuing. I might have thrown up my hands and gone back to tweeting or looking in the freezer for some forbidden food to munch on--or just plopped down in front of my over-sized TV and watched episodes of "Jeopardy" or "The Wheel of Fortune."

After successfully testing "The Improvenator," and actually seeing what my invention was capable of doing, I placed small ads in The New York Times, The Wall Street Journal, News And World Report and The Huffington Post. The reaction was beyond my wildest dreams. I don't remember the exact figures but enough "Improvenators" were purchased in those first days to warrant hiring fifty more workers and keeping our plant open on weekends.

The public quickly discovered that "The Improvenator" had what we said it had--the potential to enhance the quality of life for every man, woman and child on our planet.

I am smiling broadly as I sit at my computer and 'diarize' the good thoughts that are racing through my head. I had made the right decision about inviting friends and strangers to the private unveiling of my "Improvenator." I am not being immodest when I say that words like "blown away" and "thunderstruck" were bandied about--their words, not mine.

I am sorely tempted to divulge the names of some of the people who, that day, actually said "blown away" or "thunderstruck," but until formal contracts are signed that indemnify us from lawsuits, I can only say that on the 'Who's Who' list of celebrities who waxed eloquent after viewing my twelve-by-fifteen-by-four inch labor of love, were stars and celebrities in the same pantheon that is reserved for the likes of Mel Brooks, Norman Lear, Dick Van Dyke, Jon Stewart, Stephen Hawking, Bill Maher, Billy Crystal, Rachel Maddow, Jerry Seinfeld, Chris Rock, Conan O'Brien, Queen Latifah, Jimmy Kimmel, Kevin Nealon, Tom

Bergeron, Jimmy Fallon, Ellen DeGeneres, Julie Chen, Sara Gilbert, Sharon Osbourne, Aisha Tyler, Sheryl Underwood, Charlie Rose, Neil Simon, Rob Reiner, Oprah Winfrey, Stephen Colbert, Chris Matthews, Joy Behar, Robin Roberts, Amy Robach, George Stephanopoulos, Lara Spencer, Christiane Amanpour, Kathie Lee Gifford, Hoda Kotb, Savannah Guthrie, Natalie Morales, Matt Lauer, Tavis Smiley, Betty White, Andrea Mitchell, Paul Reiser, Harry Belafonte, Bill & Hillary Clinton, Barack and Michelle Obama, Sarah Silverman--and others of that ilk.

Regular folk who do not worry about lawsuits or their status are freely heaping similar words of praise on my 'brainchild.' Most are astounded to learn that "The Improvenator," which retails for $69.99, has a lifetime guarantee, with a warranty that states: "If, for any reason, your improvenator is stolen or lost, it will be replaced, free of charge.

I realize that I have not fully explained why I am so gung-ho about "The Improvenator." You may think I am singing its praises because it is my brainchild, but I daresay that after owning one, you may feel I have not sung its praises loudly enough.

I think it may be helpful if, instead of enumerating the many functions which the "Improvenator" is capable of performing, I list the functions that this miraculous item cannot perform--it will, I assure you, be an infinitely shorter list. I was about to start the list by noting that my creation will not be capable of babysitting your children, but immediately realized that, in some instances, "The Improvenator" could be a godsend.

What my device can do is faithfully copy any document that exists.

I am aware of what some free spirits may be thinking and I hasten to inform you that The Improvenator can print money, but it no longer will. Our nation's Treasury Department insisted that we also edit out the device's ability to print treasury bills or postage stamps.

Now, as to the extraordinary things your miracle device can do for you, I offer you a list. To get optimum results, I suggest you carefully read the simple but important directions that are printed in our suede covered instruction book.

A word of warning! Be wary of anyone advertising the sale of a "New and Improved Improvenator." Even if it were true, you will have no need for it, for embedded in our "Improvenator" is a 'Self-Improvement' feature that will kick in any time your "Improvenator" is asked to solve a problem that, heretofore, never existed. Below is a small sample of items that your "Improvenator" is geared to do.

It can improve:

Your health.
Your looks.
Your sex life.
Your life extpectancy.
The conscience of right wing GOP lawmakers.
All nations' abilities to solve problems without weapons and wars.
Government actions that prohibit the fouling of our atmosphere.
The building of roads, bridges, dams and infrastructures.
Your compulsion to eat things you know will keep you up at night.
Your memory, so that you don't forget to take your pills.
Your memory, so that you don't take your pills twice.

FYI: Major news networks have recently reported that the following countries are presently marketing counterfeit "Improvenators.":

China has just announced a device they call, "The Improperprober."

Russia is gearing up to manufacture –"The Interproovocat."

India has already started to peddle a device called "The Improcreator."

And in Japan they are said to be on the verge of flooding the world markets with their "The Imbabahnazaito."

Buyers Beware!

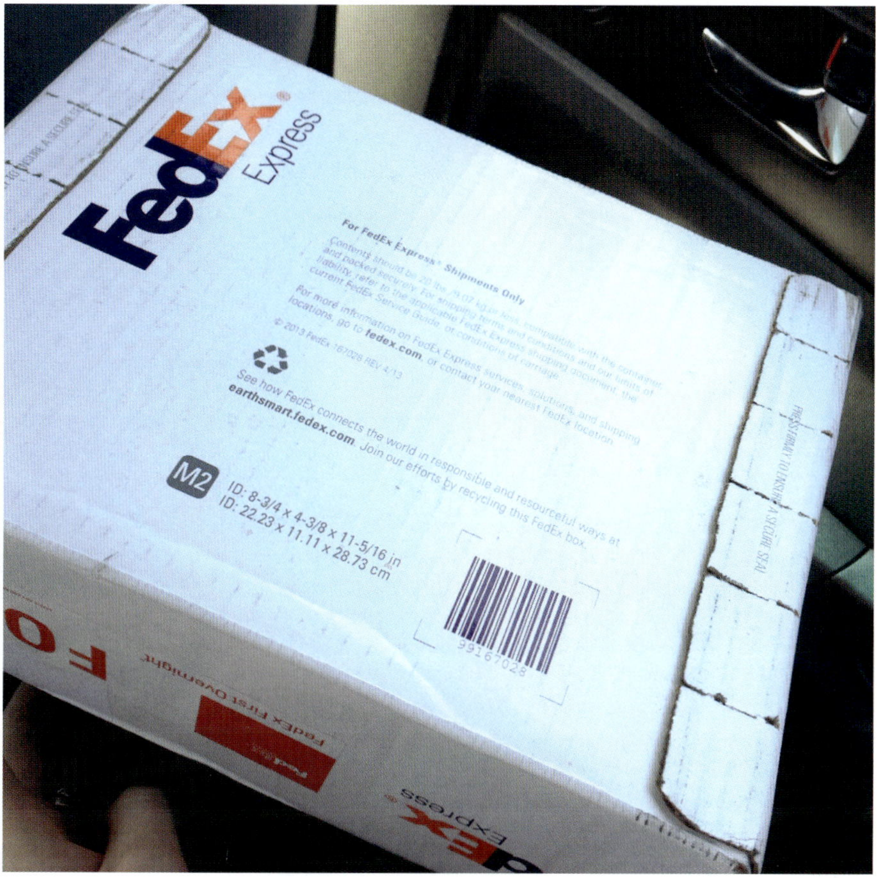

My Improventaor delivered to you by FedEx.

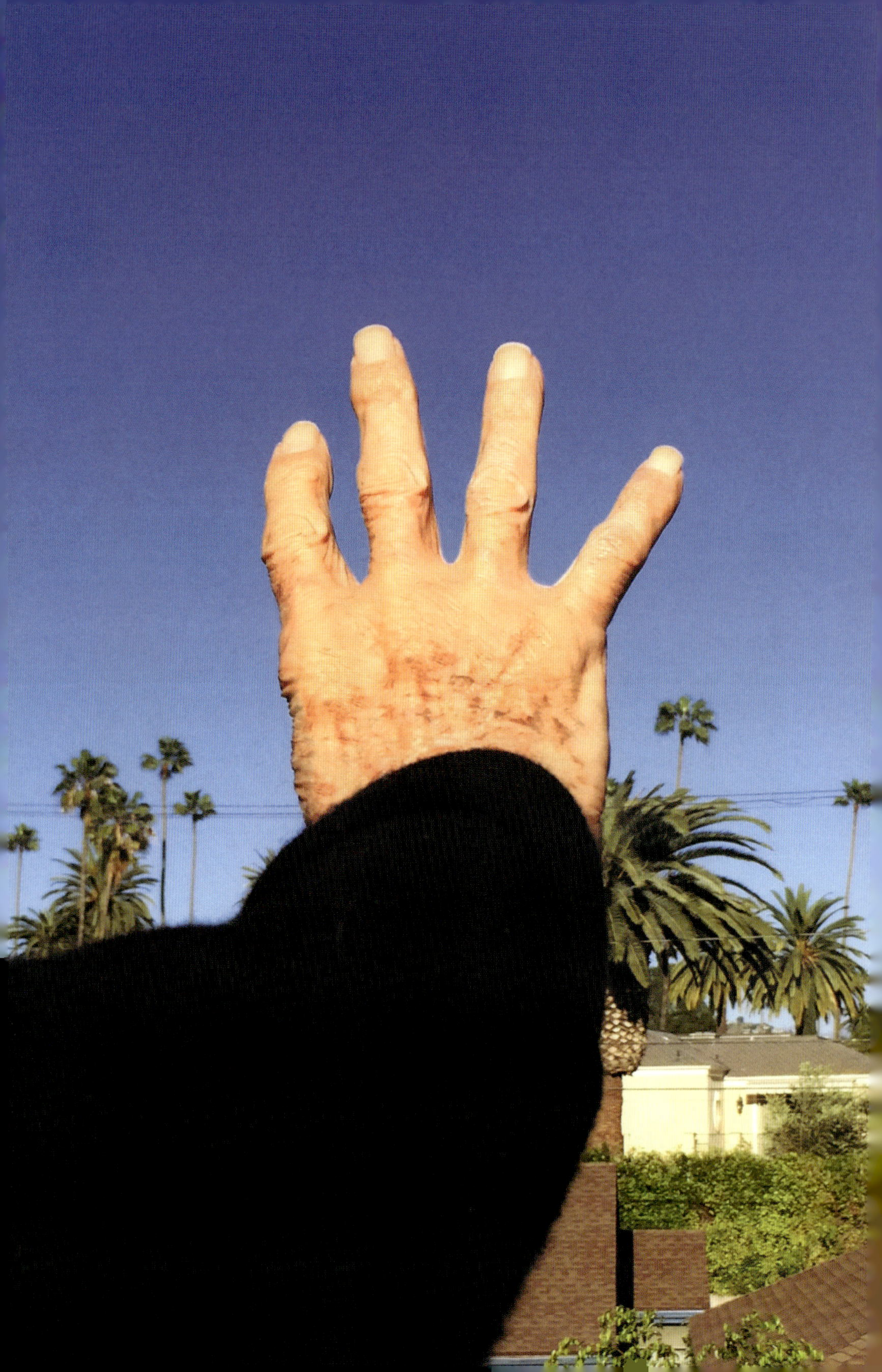

Four ‘Synchronistic’ Incidents I Have Experienced

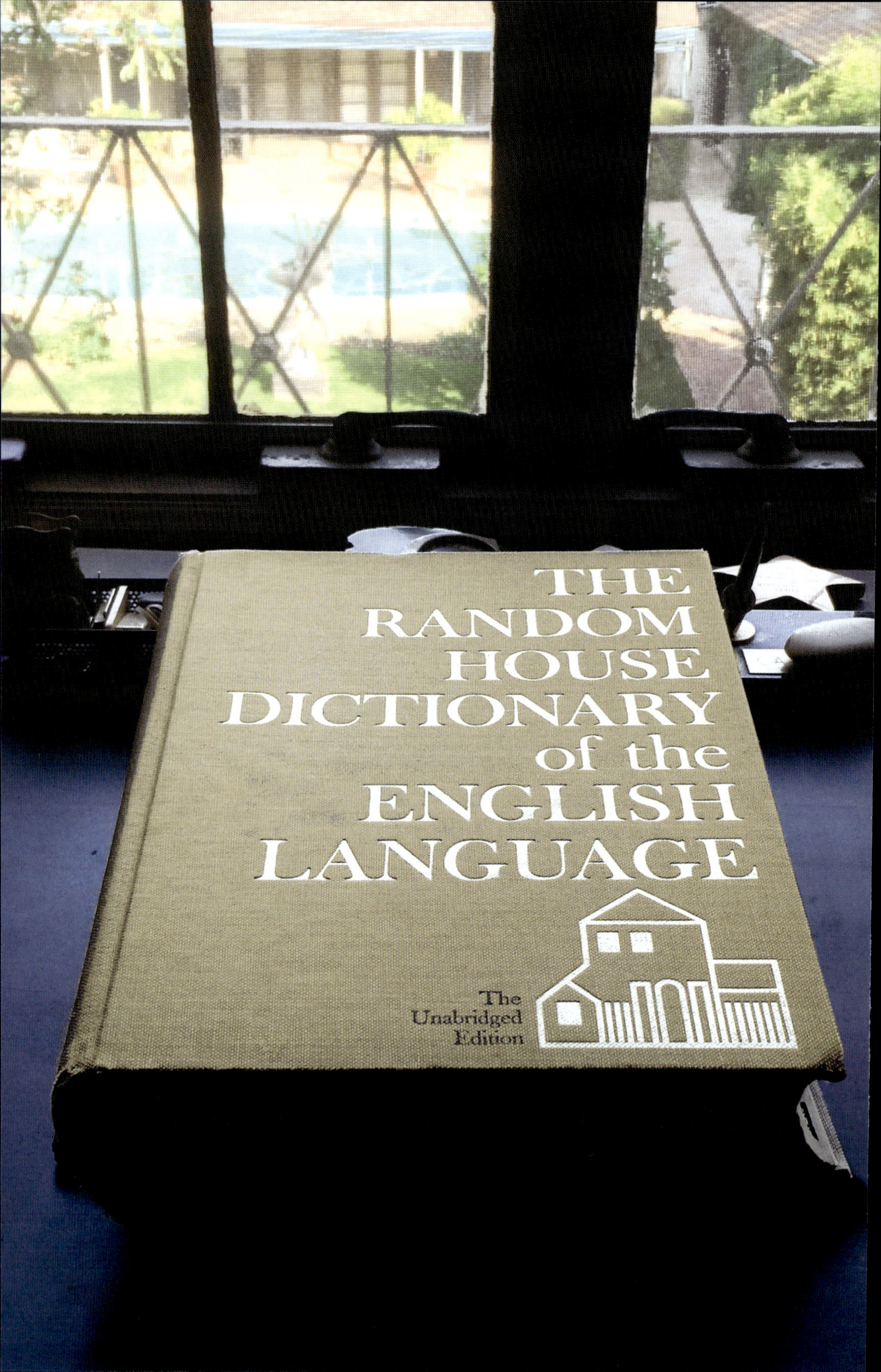
THE
RANDOM
HOUSE
DICTIONARY
of the
ENGLISH
LANGUAGE
The
Unabridged
Edition

CHAPTER FIVE

Four 'Synchronistic' Incidents I Have Experienced

After titling this chapter, I grabbed my 1943 Webster's Dictionary, looked up synchronistic and did not find the word. I found synchronic, synchroneity, synchronized and synchronism and decided that my word, 'synchronistic,' more accurately describes the four contiguous events of which I was a part. I do hope that some forward thinking lexicographer who, when preparing new editions of their dictionary, considers adding the word 'synchronistic.'

Whoa, whoa! I just learned from my publisher, who was peering over my shoulder, that 'synchronistic' is, indeed, a word and he proved it by opening my too-heavy-to-lift "Random House Dictionary's Unabridged Edition of the English Language," which he had lugged to my desk. The 1943 edition of Webster's dictionary, which was compiled and edited by Noah Webster himself, was the one responsible for my gaffe.

As to the four synchronistic moments, I vaguely recall relating two of the three of these moments but I am not sure if I was telling someone about it or writing about it in an earlier book. Before going to print or maybe as early as later this evening, I will look through all my previously published works and see whether or not I am plagiarizing myself.

I know for certain that the one 'synchronistic' moment that I have never written about but have told to a couple of friends, happened about a week ago. It was about 10 A.M. and I was lying in bed, watching television and doing my daily stretches. I was counting out loud as I did a series of sit-ups and at the exact moment I grunted "eleven," a woman on my TV set said "eleven." It was the co-host of "Lingo," Shandi Finnessy who had said it and was holding a billiard-sized ball that had an eleven printed on it. I had been watching a re-re-rerun of "Lingo," the game show hosted by Chuck Woolery. I have no way of computing the odds of a person saying "eleven," or any number, at the precise moment he sees and hears another person say it, but I will bet it is in the million-to-one-shot category.

Shandi Finnessy & Chuck Woolery

The first synchronistic moment I recall experiencing was in the summer of 1971. My wife Estelle and I were happily ensconced in a Malibu Beach house that our dear friends Ruth and Gil Kraft had invited us to use for a couple of weeks and it was a pleasant sojourn-except for one morning.

The morning I speak of was in the kitchen, right after I loaded our dirty breakfast dishes into the dishwasher and shoved some orange rinds into the sink's garbage disposal unit. I then, simultaneously, flicked the on-switch of both appliances, and a split second later the ground beneath us started to tremble and my wife screamed,

"Carl! An earthquake--- get away from the window!!"

"Honey, its not an earthquake, it's me! I did it!" I laughed as I stumbled from the sink, "I shouldn't have switched on the dishwasher and garbage disposal at the same time! I'll turn them off!"

I managed to keep my balance as I ran back to the sink and turned off both appliances which, to my surprise, did not stop anything! It took another few seconds until the earthquake, which was centered in Sylmar, stopped its quaking.

My wife, though frightened, managed a smile and said, "Thank you dear. Promise me you won't start any more earthquakes!"

I did promise and since that day, I have not, started any or taken credit for, any of the earthquakes that, periodically test our nerves. Quite the contrary, the other day, while standing in the street in front of my house, my assistant, Bess said, "Hey, did you feel that tremor?"

"What tremor?" I asked.

I was not kidding. At my age, I am not that steady on my feet and at the moment before the ground moved, I was catching my balance, thus negating the small tremor on the San Andreas Fault.

Anent self-plagiary:

From a shelf, I picked up my very first bio, "My Anecdotal Life," and found two synchronistic stories that I had planned to use for this chapter, and by gum, with the author's permission and blessing, I hasten to include them.

For those few who did not read my 2003 bio, here is an edited version of what I had written in a chapter titled, "Two Weird Coincidences."

I was eighteen years old and a resident member of "The Rochester Summer Theater" in Avon, New York. One evening after dinner the members of our company were relaxing in the front parlor of our sedate rooming house, listening to a radio program called "Professor Quiz." Professor Quiz would walk through the audience with a hand mike and ask someone a random question which, if answered correctly, would earn that

I had just come out of my room and, as I made my way down a flight of stairs, I announced confidently, "The answer to Professor Quiz's next question is Mickey Cochrane!" I stopped and stared when I heard the Professor ask, "Sir, for ten dollars, can you tell me the name of the catcher for the Detroit Tigers?"

"Mickey Cochrane!" the man blurted out.

Our room became eerily silent.

Me and fellow actors at Rochester Summer Theater's boardinghouse

I was just as shocked as they were but chose not to show it. When asked, "How did you do that?" I smiled, shrugged and walked on.

'*Who does it hurt,*' I thought, '*if my fellow actors think I have occult powers?*'

The fourth synchronistic story I cadged from "My Anecdotal Life" involved my son Lucas who, by the way, established art critics have described as "an original and brilliant artist."

A few years ago, Lucas phoned to ask me about where his Grandpa had been born and I told him the name of the small city in the Austro-Hungarian empire. My son then asked me to spell the city's name and I said, "I'm not sure but I think it's spelled "C-H-E-R-N-O-W-I-T-Z ." At that point, the doorbell rang and I told Lucas to hold while I went to see who was at the door.

It was the mailman, who handed me a package which I unwrapped as I made my way back to the phone. It was a book entitled "Faith, Hope and Courage," by Arthur Spitzer.

I picked up the phone and said, "Luke, I just gave you one way to spell Chernowitz–but in Europe the preferred spelling is C-Z-E-R-N-O-W-I-T-Z."

I then continued to give him a history of the town, when and how, after being annexed by Germany, it became part of Romania. I kept on until Lucas stopped me with, "Hey Dad, where are you getting all this information from?"

"From a book on Czernowitz." I answered calmly. "It just arrived by mail."

He laughed! He thought I was joking and it took me a few minutes to convince him that we were both party to a mind blowing coincidence.

I wonder what the odds are that I would get this information a few seconds after my son asked for it? I'd venture that they are at least a gadzillion to one–give or take a quintillion.

To explain how and why that particular book came to my door:

Years earlier, a gent I met at a dinner party mentioned that he was born in 'Czernowitz.' When I told him that it was my father's birthplace, he said that he was writing a book about the city and, if ever it was published, he would present me with a copy. And three years later he did. I received a copy of "Faith Hope and Courage," which the author had inscribed, "Enjoy!"

I did enjoy it, but not as much as I enjoyed having such a super synchronistic tale to tell.

PLAN
von
CZERNOWITZ
mit Angabe der neuen Strassenbenennung.
Nach amtlichen Aufzeichnungen zusammengestellt
vom städt. Baubeamten
LEON KREINER
Verlag v. Romuald Schally, Czernowitz.
VORSTADT KLOKUCZKA
VORSTADT KALICZANKA
VORSTADT ROSCH
VORSTADT MANASTERISKA
aerarische
Weidenpflanzung
städt. Weidenpflanzung
städt. Wiese
Bahnhof
Schlachthaus
Austria-Platz
Exercier-Platz
Artillerie-Kaserne
Beilage zu Mittelmanns illustrierten Führer durch die Bukowina

Tyrone Power, My Handsomest Co-Star Ever

Chi-Chi
PALM SPRINGS,
SAIPAN

CHAPTER SIX

Tyrone Power, My Handsomest Co-Star Ever

This morning, when cramming some potentially worthwhile papers into the bottom drawer of my desk, my eye was caught by a small, dog-eared folder on which was a photo of a topless model and the words "Chi-Chi Starlite Room." A Palm Springs club that my wife and relatives had visited years ago. Inside the folder I found an eclectic bunch of photos, among them, my Mom and Pop, a photo of me holding my Mark Twain prize, a color snap shot of Livia, my then three year old, red-haired granddaughter, my Mom at twenty-five, shepherding my nattily dressed four year old brother Charlie. I found too, a somewhat blurry snapshot of me and Tyrone Power the impetus for writing this chapter.

I had not seen that blurry photo in years and thought that because it was so 'illegible' someone may have tossed it out. It is, of course, the photo of Tyrone Power and me. Now, whether or not your interest is piqued, if you turn the page, you will have the opportunity to see that blurry photo that another famous person snapped fifty-nine years ago.

TYRONE POWER ME

SAIPAN 45

I am aware that there are some young moviegoers who have heard of Tyrone Power, but I am guessing that an equal amount may never have heard of him or seen any of his films. For the latter and for my own pleasure, I offer you a partial list of the forty films in which he starred.

The Mark Of Zorro, Blood and Sand, A Yank In The R.A.F., The Sun Also Rises, The Razor's Edge, Nightmare Alley, Captain From Castille, Witness For The Prosecution, Lloyds of London, and Alexander's Ragtime Band. Tyrone Power's career started in 1936 and ended when he passed away in 1958, at the age of forty-four.

Once again I, a registered Atheist, am willing to swear on a stack of Bibles or The Complete Works of Mark Twain and William Shakespeare, that what I am about to tell you may sound unbelievable but it is absolutely true!!

In chapter seven of this bio, I wrote of four 'synchronistic' moments that I had experienced in my lifetime. Well, today I had a fifth.

At 11PM last night the last words I had written were the title of Tyrone Power's final film, "Solomon And Sheba," and at 11AM this morning, in the Arts Section of the Los Angeles Times, I saw a publicity photo of Tyrone Power and Alice Faye in "Alexander's Ragtime Band." The article told of the plans that Tyrone Power's children, Taryn and Tyrone Jr., had to mount a tribute to their father at the Hollywood Museum.

I thought immediately about the faded photo I have of their Dad and me that was taken in Saipan by another actor, Howard Duff, who, on radio, had a five year run playing detective Sam Spade and after the war had a happy thirty-three year marriage to beautiful Ida Lupino.

At the time I was performing in "Shape Ahoy," Captain Power, who ferried American built bombers to England, was having a short 'lay-over' in Saipan.

Howard Duff was then in charge of operating Saipan's radio station which broadcast news, played popular songs and, on occasion, offered comedy sketches.

Fortuitously, he had a two character sketch ready to air and two actors who could play the parts. He asked Captain Power if he would play the part of an Army Captain and if I would play a character named Private Peepsight.

I'll never forget the day Tyrone Power and I stood a foot apart and faced each. I could not believe that I was sharing a microphone with Tyrone Power, one of my, and the world's, favorite actors! And best of all, we seemed to work well together! I found a goofy voice for Private Peepsight and, after a quick read through, we went on the air. Judging by the reaction of the crew, who laughed at every line I delivered, and Captain Power telling me that I gave "a "splendid performance," I was ecstatic and immediately wrote to tell Estelle about whom I'd met!

And the unexpected thrill of having the photo of us that Howard Duff took –and my sending it home to my wife! The photo that, sixty-nine years later, spurred this chapter.

If I may, and who's going to stop me, I'd like to re-write the line about meeting Tyrone Power: 'I will never forget that day,' and have it read, "I will never, ever, ever, ever forget that day!"

Howard Duff as Sam Spade

GUINNESS WORLD RECORDS™

Campaign for Inclusion in The Guinness Book Of World Records

"Hot In Cleveland" cast: Carl Reiner, Wendy Malick, Betty White, Valerie Bertinelli & Jane Leeves

CHAPTER SEVEN

Campaign for Inclusion in The Guinness Book Of World Records

A few months ago I made a guest appearance on the long running and very popular television series, "Hot In Cleveland," which boasts a cast of lovely and talented women that includes Valerie Bertinelli, Wendie Malick, Jane Leeves and Betty White. On this episode I played Max, a charming old gent (not too much of a stretch) who courts Elka, a character played by the indomitable and beloved Betty White.

I have known of Betty White and her illustrious career long before she married Allen Ludden, the smiley host of the popular game show, "Password." During World War II, I knew of Allen Ludden as Captain Ludden, the tad less smiley officer-in-charge of the entertainment unit to which I had been assigned. It is for that reason I now refer to Betty White as my "Captain-in-law."

Capt. Allen Ludden & Carl Reiner

Betty White & Allen Ludden

While walking back from the set of "Hot In Cleveland," after being charming in our small but effective scene, Betty told me that "The Guinness Book Of World Records" was planning to include her in their forthcoming edition. It seems that, no other female performer has had a longer career in television—a career that, bless her, is still ongoing. In 1949, an enterprising TVstation started focused their cameras on her and started telecast her performances.

Hearing this statistic, I started to recall my early days in the medium and, whaddya know, it may well be that I too am eligible for inclusion in the Guinness Book of World Records as TV's oldest, longest active male performer.

Between 1946 and 1948, I appeared on three of these following shows, "The Maggie McNellis Crystal Room," "The Earl Wrightson Show," a variety show that starred who else, but the popular baritone, Earl Wrightson, and the third was "The Fashion Story" in which I co-starred with Marilyn Day, a lovely and talented singer.

Earl Wrightson

I Googled the names of those shows to check the correct dates and histories and it took all of five minutes to learn that both "The Maggie McNellis Crystal Room" and "The Earl Wrightson Show" had short, unhappy lives in 1948 and 1949 respectively, and "The Marilyn Day Show" had a happier but not much longer life in the 1947-48 seasons. What I did learn is that having performed in 1947 and 1948 gives me a fairly strong leg to stand on if I decide to request my name be included in the next "Guinness Book Of World Records."

I remember receiving a hundred dollars for performing my act on the Maggie McNellis and Earl Wrightson shows. I realized that when I did my act in a small club, no more than fifty to a hundred people saw it, but when I performed it on television, many thousands did, and among them might well be a club-goer who had already seen and heard me tell those jokes. Very early on, performers learned that television was a ravenous ogre that demanded fresh fare daily.

I was most happy doing "The Marilyn Day Show" even though my salary for that half-hour's work was only eighty dollars. I played the part of a fashion show photographer and delivered scripted lines that were mildly amusing. I also enjoyed Marilyn Day's excellent singing and interacting with a bevy of beautiful fashion models was not a hardship.

For me, 1948 was a good year financially. Not only was I earning eighty dollars for doing "The Fashion Story," but I was making another hundred-and-fifty appearing in a Broadway show, "Inside U.S.A." It starred Bea Lillie and Jack Haley, who had played 'The Tin Man' in "The Wizard of Oz." Besides appearing in two sketches, I also understudied Mr. Haley and worked hard to learn all the lyrics to the tricky rhyming songs, but never got a chance to do the part. The one time Mr. Haley took sick, he insisted on 'going on!'

"I will never," Mr. Haley explained, "never disappoint an audience who paided good money to see me perform."

To illustrate how young the television industry was when I entered it, I have but to describe the studio from whence "The Fashion Show" originated. It was telecast by ABC whose New York studio was then, and still is, located on West 67th Street, off Central Park West. I will never forget entering the building and making my way to their one-and-only studio. To get to the small, padded, sound-proofed room I had to walk around a former indoor horse training facility. There was sawdust on the earthen floor where horses' hooves had only recently stopped stomping. A faint aroma of manure was still present. The only other show that emanated from that ABC Studio was "The Nightly News with Doug Edwards."

I would be proud as punch to be included in "The Guinness Book Of World Records," as is my lovely "Captain-in-law," Betty White!

Hugh Jackman Owes Bobby Van Who Owes Gordon Reid, and King

CHAPTER EIGHT

Hugh Jackman Owes Bobby Van Who Owes Gordon Reid, and King

Just two nights ago I found myself shouting at one of the single most talented men in show business. It was Sunday night and my buddy Mel Brooks and I were watching the 2014 Tony Awards when Hugh Jackman, nattily attired in a tuxedo, hopped his way up and down the streets of New York, to historic Radio City Music Hall, into the theater's ornate lobby, through the foyer, down the aisle of the vast auditorium, up onto the great stage, and stopped hopping his way when he had decided that the audience had gotten his message.

During this time Hugh was hopping his way to the Music Hall, I matched him shout for hop, yelling, "Bobby Van! Bobby Van, Bobby Van"

Bobby Van had done that same kind of hopping in..in..the movie—oooh, what the hell's the name of that movie...? Hugh Jackman is stealing that routine from Bobby Van ...it was in that movie where Bobby hopped through the streets of a small town! Damn, what was that movie!?"

I was happy to stop yelling "Bobby Van! Bobby Van!" when Hugh tacitly acknowledged Bobby as the original "hopper" by passing and saluting a video screen that displayed a recording of Bobby Van's hopping!

A year or so before Bobby appeared in that film, whose title I will find, I had appeared with Bobby on Broadway in a show called "Alive and Kicking." I performed in comedy sketches and Bobby did a solo tap dance that closed the first act.

From the very first out-of-town tryout, Bobby never received less than a solid round of applause. Our choreographer, the acclaimed dancer, Michael Kidd, created the dances for the show which included a brilliant ballet for our sexy ballerina, Valerie Bettis. He left the choreography for Bobby's number to Bobby's Dad, Harry King. Harry was a former vaudevillian who toured as a member of the "flash dance" trio, "Gordon, Reid and King."

I remember Bobby's Dad say something that I have never forgotten. It was during the out-of-town previews for "Alive And Kicking" that rehearsals were scheduled to work on improving two of the sketches. Time was also allotted for Bobby Van to rehearse his number which, night after night, had been a sure-fire crowd-pleaser.

"Mr. King," I asked, naively, "why does Bobby have to rehearse? He stops the show every night!"

"Yes, but not long enough!" Mr. King asserted.

"But the audience loves him-- he has to take two curtain calls, what can be better?"

"Three curtain calls!"

After hours of work, Mr. King devised a flashier finish to his son's solo and, for the rest of the run, the appreciative audiences never let Bobby leave the stage before he took at least three curtain calls.

I asked Google, whose memory is so much better than mine to give me the name of the film in which Bobby Van did a specialty dance number where he hopped all over a small town, and the answer came back, "Small Town Girl," released in 1953.

Google also coughed up Bobby Van performing two of the most graceful and spectacular song-and-dance sequences ever done on film. Those sequences were equal to those danced by the likes of Fred Astaire, Gene Kelley, Donald O'Connor, Bob Fosse and Tommy Rall.

One Bobby Van number is entitled "Take Me To Broadway" and the other, "My Flaming Heart." If you enjoy brilliance, ask Google to play for you what it just played for me.

It is sad to note that Robert Jack Stein, AKA Bobby Van, born in the Bronx in 1928 and happily married to the lovely and talented Elaine Joyce, was with us for only fifty-two years before making his final exit.

Bobby Van bouncing in "Small Town Girl"

Me, Milton Berle and the Exotic Silent Film Star, Pola Negri

CHAPTER NINE

Me, Milton Berle and the Exotic Silent Film Star, Pola Negri

I believe that it was in 1952 that I had the privilege to meet with Pola Negri, who from 1914 to 1964 reigned as the world's most glamorous actresses of the silent film era. The five foot tall Miss Negri had torrid romances with the greatest silent film comedian, Charlie Chaplin, and the greatest silent film lover, Rudolph Valentino.

In her latter years, the Polish born actress, who had starred in at least sixty European and American motion pictures, now scaled back her film appearances and appeared in person at the country's major vaudeville theaters.

I was told by Harry Kalcheim, my rep at the William Morris Agency, that Miss Negri had planned to mount a show on Broadway, and I had absolutely no idea what, if anything, I might contribute to her show, which consisted of her singing, dancing and relating stories about her life. I was intrigued with the prospect of meeting a film star whom my parents had held in high regard.

Mr. Kalcheim was asked to escort me to her apartment, which was a huge, Park Avenue penthouse.

Mr. Kalcheim and I were ushered into a living room that looked very much like an upscale movie set. I had expected that Miss Negri would make a grand entrance, but instead found her standing in front of colorful drapes, dressed in a flowing, white gown and staring into space.

Without acknowledging our presence, she lifted her well coiffed head, showed us her pretty profile and, with her hand on her hip, welcomed us.

"Mr. Reiner," she said in a throaty, Polish-accented voice, "Do you know why you are here?"

"I think to read for a part in your new Broadway show?"

"Not at all," she explained, "I am not looking for an actor to play a part. I am looking for a Confrencier and I was told that you are an excellent Confrencier. Are you?"

Having studied French in the Army, I was guessing that Confrencier had to do with hosting or emceeing and I guessed right. I told her that I consider myself "a rather good Confrencier."

Miss Negri went on to describe how,between numbers when she left the stage to change costumes, she needed someone "to amuse the audience with jokes and funny stories."

She asked if I would be interested in such a job and when I politely lied that it sounded like "an interesting challenge," she said that I should "think about it."

We said our good-byes and left. Our meeting with Miss Negri took less than three minutes and we needed but three seconds to know that there was nothing to 'think about.' In the elevator, we looked at each other and shrugged.

Pola Negri never mounted that show, but my meeting her was fortuitous, as it jogged a memory of an encounter with Milton Berle who provided a good punch line to this chapter... a quotable one.

Milton Berle, who was credited as being the man responsible for the sale of millions of television sets, reigned as the King of Television from 1948 to 1956. "Mr. Television," as he was dubbed by the press, was born in 1908 and passed away in 2002. In those ninety-four years, he successfully performed in every decade of his life and in every show biz venue that exists, from vaudeville, radio and night clubs to Broadway, television and motion pictures.

It was at a chance meeting at some event that Milton Berle and I found ourselves chatting about the business and, for some reason, comparing notes about Pola Negri. I told him of my confusing and very short interview with the great lady and he told me of how they had met when he was a callow youth of twenty and she was an alluring woman of thirty-three. It was at the time that Miss Negri was touring the country doing her vaudeville act and Milton was the resident Master of Ceremonies at the Palace Theater in New York City.

Milton was quite taken by her beauty but, knowing his place, he did not make any of his patented moves on her. At the end of her run at the Palace, Miss Negri graciously invited Milton to her Park Avenue penthouse to share "a farewell drink."

Pola Negri

Milton Berle

In the living room of her lavish apartment, he said that they sat together on a plush sofa and chatted about the theater and their careers.

Milton described her as someone who was not only "really, really beautiful" but that she also "smelled nice."

He said that he would have liked to have made a move on her but his better judgment kept him from doing so.

After awhile, he wondered if she might possibly be amenable to his getting amorous-- but again, dismissed the thought.

After the third or fourth drink, Milton said that Miss Negri daintily blotted her nose with a hanky and purred, "Milton it is so stifling in here–be a dear open the drapes and allow some fresh air into the apartment."

He did so and sat down next to her, wondering whether she would toss him out on his ear if he did 'make a move on her.' While considering his options, he said that Pola Negri looked out the window and without looking at him, took a deep breath and gushed, "Ahhh, New York! What a magnificent skyline-- and look at our beautiful Empire State building!

"Milton, does it not remind you of a great big cock!?"

It was then Milton knew what he had to do! Seconds later he happily followed Miss Negri into her lavish bedroom where the notoriously well endowed Milton Berle made his move. With his eager endowment he pleasured the great international star.

And I was pleasured that Milton Berle chose me to be the chronicler of this charismatic coupling.

99¢ only STORES
1155
VALENTINE'S DAY!
Save More...
Shop Us First!
got ice?
7lbs
BALLOONS
Mylar

99 Cents Stores: Most Appreciated by The Poor & Nouveau Riche

open 9 days a week
HANKS
& CREDIT CARDS

CHAPTER TEN

99 Cents Stores: Most Appreciated by The Poor & Nouveau Riche

With our first sight of the new store whose sign boldly announced that none of their items cost more than ninety-nine cents, my wife and I sang out, in unison, "Hey, that's for us!"

Having been poor as children and having decades earlier become Nouveau Riche (newly rich), we made a right turn off Sunset Boulevard and into the 99¢ Store parking lot.

In their massive windows were displayed some of the wares that could be bought for the announced price. Many items such as lip balm, a book light, a pair of plastic gloves, Comet cleanser, a high fashion necklace and a plastic collapsible water pitcher, were on sale for less than 99 cents.

Recently I visited the 99¢ Store where Estelle and I often made our way up and down every one of the dozens of aisles-- sometimes looking, sometimes handling and continuously saying things like:

"Hey Hon, look at this!"

"Is this something we can use?"

"At that price, we don't have to use it."

"Wow! 99 cents for a tennis racket!"

"Hey are these crackers real Saltines?"

"Honey, we could use some of that Christmas wrapping paper."

" Two bags of Bosc pears for 99 cents? Now that's a bargain."

"Not if they're squishy."

"Could that canned spaghetti be good?"

"Take one and we'll find out!"

"Take three in case they're good"

"Don't you need bedroom slippers?"

"Yes, but not bunny ones."

That day Estelle and I saved money, and today I saved paper by writing a one page chapter!

The Straight Pin

The Straight Pin, Literature's Most Ignored and Essential Commodity

34/35
NON-IRON

CHAPTER ELEVEN

The Straight Pin, Literature's Most Ignored and Essential Commodity

For many centuries there have been thousands of great, mediocre and trashy novels written by as many great, mediocre and trashy novelists. These dedicated scriveners have covered a myriad of subjects and all manner of people--from kings to commoners, from cops to cop killers, from lovers to lawyers, from private-eyes to public menaces, from masochists to sadists, from bridge builders to bridge players, from cross bearers to cross-dressers and from zoo keepers to zombies.

I tell you all this because last night a thought pricked my mind as I was in the process of removing one of the half dozen little straight pins that kept my new white dress shirt neatly folded and moored to a slab of thin cardboard. A second after my mind was pricked with that thought, my finger was pricked by a straight pin. I cursed the shiny culprit who, along with his sharp tipped buddies, I was about to toss into a wastebasket.

"Hey," my pricked mind thought, "do you know where these pins belong?"

"Yes," I nodded internally, "in Estelle's faded red pin cushion that's shaped like a ripe tomato."

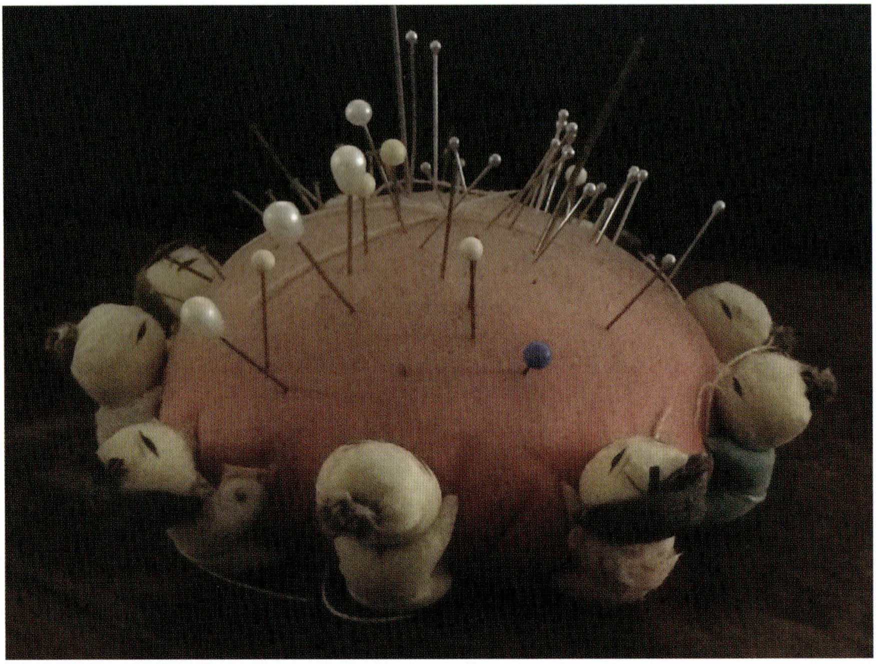

Through the years, that faded cushion had become a resting place for errant sewing needles and for a raft of straight pins. My mother Bessie, and my mother-in-law Minnie, owned similarly laden pin cushions.

I could not have pricked my finger at a more opportune time, as I had just finished writing the last chapter and, for this chapter I was struggling to find an original subject to skewer.

As I dabbed a Kleenex tissue at the minuscule drop of blood on the tip of my forefinger, I thought,'*Hey, this stupid straight pin! What could be more fun to skewer than a thing that is, in itself, a bonafide skewer? The straight pin! How fortuitous that I stuck myself with one of them!*'

I looked at the shank of the sharply pointed metal item in my hand and I wondered, "*Has any author, little known or famous, ever written a serious essay or short story where its cental character is a straight pin? And if they had, was it published? Who cares! I don't know, but what I do know is that it is worth a shot and, damn it, I am going to try creating such a tale– and right now-- and I'll dedicate it to a boyhood chum who grew up to be a member of the American Medical Association, Dr. Byron J. Winner.*"

The Discovery

The historic event I am about to describe occurred in the year 3711. I will, as succinctly as I can, describe a series of happenings that will, no doubt, seem unlikely and other-worldly, but I ask you to suspend your disbelief as you read the next few pages which, I assure you, will be both entertaining and illuminating.

Just a few short months before the dawn of the year 3711, great scientific minds, toiling in the world's great medical research laboratories and pharmaceutical facilities, made a startling discovery, a discovery that made it unlikely for any human on our planet to die from anything but natural causes. Of course, many did die of unnatural causes before their 144 year life expectancy was reached. More often, their deaths were attributed to unnatural causes such as major wars that were designed by major madmen.

In an earlier time, during the 1930's and 1940's, it would be Adolph Hitler, the maddest of madman who held the record for orchestrating the deaths of twelve million souls. Following him throughout the decades, were a few caring world leaders, but interspersed was an assortment of monsters who tied, and in some case surpassed Der Fuhrer's dubious record. To name a few:

Premier Gunner Forya Jr. of Gowanna, who, in 2999, boasted a four year killing spree that took the lives of half the population of two neighboring European nations.

In 3060, President Assassio Cadavara of the Rattatan Republic ordered that every citizen, male and female, who voted for his opponent serve no less than fifteen years in a federal prison.

In 3300, Mamakah Pusha became the Prime Minister of the emerging Asian nation Bonoco when Bonoco's sitting Prime Minister accidently drank a lethal dose of poisoned Pouilly-Fuisse.

On January first in the year 3632, Chancellor Miguel Misfortuniac slaughtered every member of the opposition party. One month later the Chancellor, while in the shower attempting to wash his sins away was shot in the heart by his cardiologist, Dr. Dono DeCriminala.

Misfortuniac's successor, Chancelor DeCriminala, who reigned until 3670, was responsible for more unnatural deaths than all of the five murdering monsters who preceded him.

On Halloween eve in the year 3702, Dono De Criminala committed suicide or so claimed by his third wife Lucia Lucio De Criminala.

Nine months after the unsolved murder of De Criminala, a period of unexpected quietude settled on our tortured planet. Its beleaguered citizens started to breathe fresh, unpolluted air and no one could fathom what had caused the Earth's toxicity to suddenly evaporate.

By the Spring of 3703, the planet had so changed that its happy and prosperous six billion inhabitants had, by a landslide referendum, voted to rename our planet. A local journalist suggested that the last and the first letters of The Earth be switched and from that day,'March 20th 3703, our planet has been called"The Heart!

FORMERLY KNOWN AS "THE EARTH"

And lo and behold, the day after the renaming, life on "The Heart" started to improve for all. There were sudden climate changes–a lowering of temperatures in the tropics and sub tropics and a dramatic cessation of the ice caps melting in the Arctic and Antarctic regions.

Contiguously, there was a dramatic explosion in the size of our fish population-- from the tiniest groups of guppies to the largest pods of sharks, "The Heart" experienced an unprecedented amount of births. Whales and dolphins, caught up in the urge to become parents, made huge contributions to the ocean's population.

One year later our nation's commander in chief, President Misako Lopez Goldfarb Ling, had entrusted a group of our nation's most prestigious and accomplished scientists to search for and find cures for all of our planet's dread diseases. She invited Doctor Shirley Annya Sboda, Director of the UHO, the Universal Health Organization, to meet and discuss the developing of an antidote to the new and deadly disease that had come to light in Central America. This virulent, unfilterable, invasive virus had already claimed scores of our inhabitants and, if not checked, had the potential to wipe out the lives of every creature on our planet–from the one-celled paramecium to the multi-celled pachyderm.

Nine gestating months later, by a stroke of fate, the search for a single cell of this elusive, viral bacteria was accidently found and from it a successful anti-viral disease vaccine was mass produced.

And where, do you imagine, was this viral bacteria found and by whom? Paradoxically, it was found by a young man who had accidently pricked his finger on one of the straight pins he had just removed from his new white shirt, a garment that had been packed at a shirt factory in Shirkistan.

Fortunately for the world, harbored on the tip of that blessed straight pin was a germ that caused a strange rash to break out on the young man's back. This lad's physician, Dr. Byron J. Wynner, hoping this germ might spawn an antidote to the planet's fatal diseases, reported his findings to the world's greatest research scientists, and by a joint effort, these dedicated men fashioned a vaccine that they dubbed "Wynner One!"

The injections of 'Wynner One' into the arm of every citizen on The Heart, rid forever all of our planet's fatal disease causing bacteria.

To pay homage to Dr. Byron J. Wynner, Shirkistan's House of Parliament has erected a bronze statue of the Doctor. On it is a plaque bearing these nine lines:

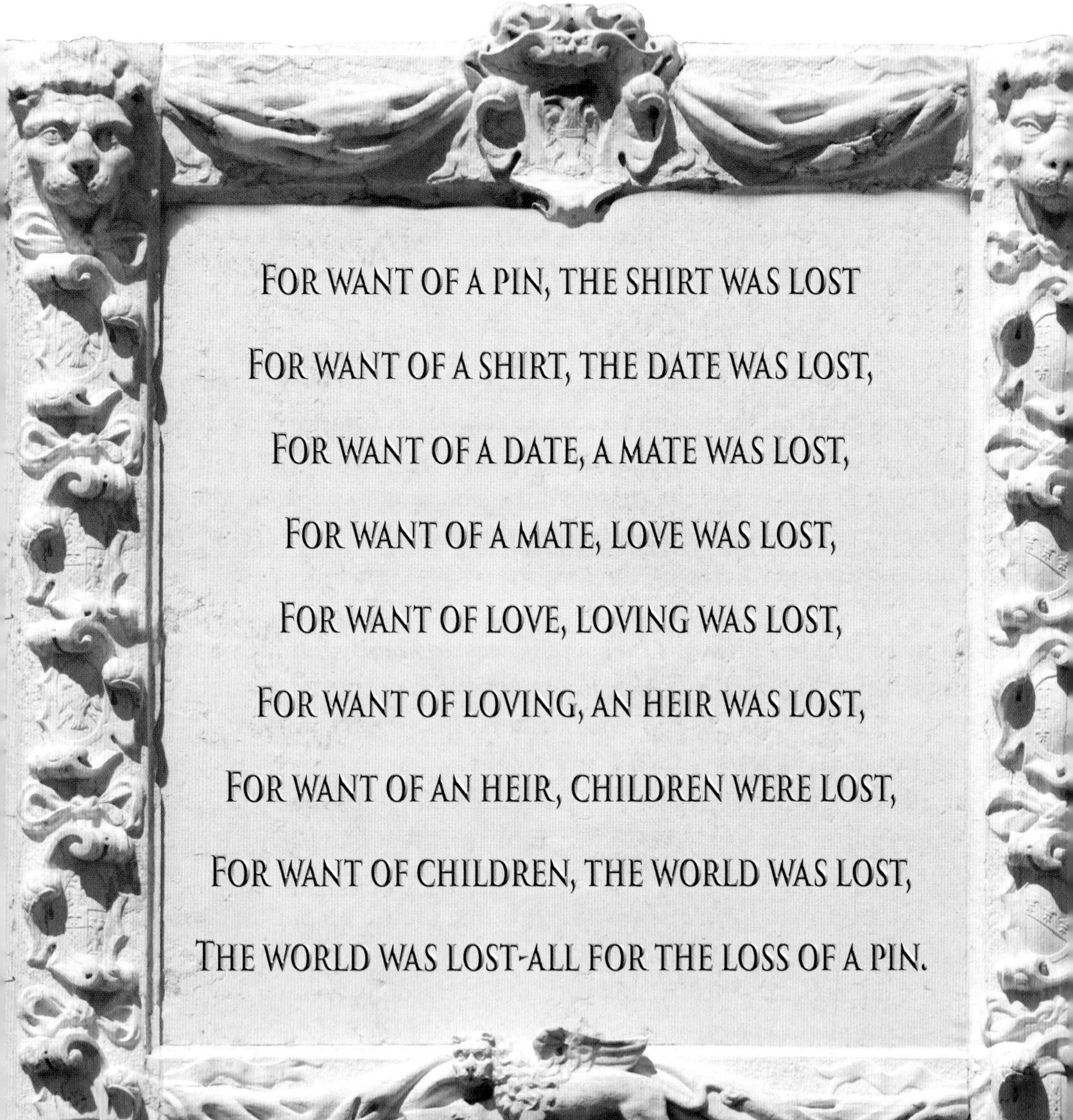

The Straight Pin That Saved The World

Sid Caeser, Howie Morris, Carl Reiner & Imogene Coco

What It Was That Brought Tears to My Eyes

Sid Caeser ~1950, "Your Show Of Shows"

CHAPTER TWELVE

What It Was That Brought Tears to My Eyes

Were it not for a heartfelt tribute that Mel Brooks, Billy Crystal and I attended at The Paley Center in Beverly Hills, honoring the memory of television's greatest comedian, Sid Caesar, I would never have known of the existence of a particular and valuable recording. It was of an appearance Mel and I made on a popular TV variety show "The Hollywood Palace," in 1965. Thanks to being computer literate, I was capable of Googling this vintage episode on YouTube. Since my long term memory loss is now competing with my short term memory loss it was invaluable in helping me remember this sketch Mel and I did.

Carl Reiner & Mel Brooks, 1965 The Hollywood Palace

That night I was not interviewing Mel Brooks as the "2000 Year Old Man" but as a 40 year old modern "tax expert" who had written a book on the subject. What was amazing to me was that watching this old recording brought tears to my eyes, eyes that do not easily tear up. Today, I require a pharmaceutical product to help me do that and that night, I might add, Mel's were somewhat watery.

Here now transcribed are the wonderfully comedic words that were being created in Mel's fertile, ad-libitum brain and pouring out of his motor-mouth- which lead to me becoming teary eyed.

We started our routine by my saying:

"Ladies and Gentlemen, as you know, tax time is soon upon us, and we are very fortunate to have secured the services of one of the great tax men of this country, Mr. Philip J. Heinker...Good evening Mr. Heinker!"

"Oh, by the way, I believe my name is Hanker."

"You pronounce it Hanker, Sir?"

"Well, that's what they call me."

"But sir, here on your book's cover, it is spelled "H e-i-n-k-e-r."

"Well then, maybe it's Heinker."

"Well, Mr. Heinker, you've written this remarkable book on taxes entitled, The Agony and the Ecstasy.

"Yes..."

"It's a rather strange title, since Mr. Irving Stone used that title for his book on Michelangelo."

"Au contraire, my dear fair! I believe Mr. Stone's title for Michelangelo was The Agony and the Ecstacasy."

"No, his book was "The Agony and the Ecstasy."

"Oh, then, mine is "The Agony and the Ectascasy." Yes that's my title..and I'm Heinker! They got it all mixed up."

"I'll call you Heinker, since your name is Heinker."

"Wait a minute, wait a minute–'Do you Philip J. Honker, take this women to be your lawful wedded..' It's Honker!"

"Okay, Mr. Honker, we are interested in knowing about your system of tax deductions. Say a man makes $100,000 a year..."

"Do you know such a man?"

"No, this person is hypothetical."

"You mean like my wife....?"

"No, no, this is not a real person, it's a hypothetical..."

"You didn't meet my wife..."

"No, it's not a real person."

"Oh, not real...it's Hollywood!...Nothing in Hollywood is real. All make believe.."

"Yes, yes..."

"Nothing is real in Hollywood...Nothing, did you know that Warner Oland is not Chinese?"

"Yes, I believe most people are aware of that."

"He was not real! He played a Chinese detective, Charlie Chan!"

"I know. Uh Sir, with your system of taxes, if a man makes $100,000 a year..."

"Do you know such a man?"

"No, I meant what would this man ordinarily pay to the Government in taxes?"

"Well, if he's a salaried employee and he earns $100,000 he would pay $90,000 of those $100,000, to his Government."

"And with your Heinker method, how much would he pay?'

"A dollar forty!"

"A dollar forty! How did you arrive at that figure?"

"Well, we do a lot of computing and figuring..."

"Legitimate computing and figuring?"

"Well, we're in court about that now..."

"You think you'll win?"

"Oh, we have a great chance of losing!"

"Ah, I see... Mr. Heinker, Hanker? Honker?

"Hold on, hold on..hold on: -'Philip J Hanker, you are dishonorably discharged from the Army'..." It's Hanker! That's it!"

"Nice to meet you–uh, Mr. Hanker...?"

"That's my name!"

"Now, you're sure it's Hanker?"

"Positive! It is Hanker!"

"So then, it is Mr. Hanker?"

"Call me Phyllis!"

"I think you mean Phillip, don't you?"

"What is it on the book cover?"

"Phillip."

"Phillip? Hmm, I am wearing a man's watch. I should have known."

"Sir, it's often been stated that you can't beat death and taxes. You've obviously done very well beating taxes by paying just a dollar forty."

"Yes, I did very well with taxes...and we're working on death now..."

"Sir, I'm very interested in finding out how you get to this figure of a dollar forty. What are some of the deductions you take?"

"Well, aside from the nation of Roumania, I..."

"You deduct the nation of Roumania?"

"Well, no one is claiming them...I send them cottage cheese and Life Magazine. They are wonderful, they're Gypsies, they're happy people. They depend on me for solemnity..."

"I see. Well, sir, besides all that...what else do you deduct?"

"I deduct my wife."

"Well, everybody deducts their wife, as an exemption."

"Not as an exemption..."

"Well then as a deduction?"

"Not as a deduction or an exemption...but as a depreciation!"

"How can you depreciate your wife?"

"You depreciate your car, don't you? You get a wrinkle in your fender, your wife gets a wrinkle in her nose, you deduct that..."

"I don't think you can."

"I can. I'm also deducting $300."

"For what?"

"For my wife's diet...she lost 30 pounds and I'm taking off $300 for that!"

"That's ten dollars a pound."

"Yes...ten dollars a pound . The price for a pound of ground chuck is a dollar seventy-five! You think ten dollars a pound for my wife isn't fair?! Look, a woman is a lovely thing. The government is depriving me of 30 pounds of happiness and flesh...where is it–if I can't hold it and touch it?!"

"One last question... Mr. Honk.. Hank.. Heink -?"

"Hold it! Uh oh -'Hinker! Hinker is my name! Now, if you'll excuse me I have to talk to David Jansen about getting my own show...like he got to do "The Fugitive." Maybe I can get a show called "The Condemned!" or, 'Hinker, Honker, Heinker- On The Lam."

What brought tears to my eyes, was seeing the smiling face of a woman in the second row. The face belonged to my beloved wife Estelle, who seemed to be honestly enjoying our performances. Another smiling woman sitting to the right of my late wife was Mel Brooks' beloved wife, the late Anne Bancroft. Now turn the page and see for yourself.

Anne Bancroft & Estelle Reiner laughing at their husbands.
The Hollywood Palace, 1965

AUTOGRAPHS

The Best of The Best

CHAPTER THIRTEEN

The Best of The Best

I first learned of this performer's existence in 1967 when she started to appear on a major Variety show hosted by Garry Moore. Instantly I became a fan as did a host of critics and TV viewers, among them hosts of critics and viewrs. It was seeing and enjoying her perform on The Garry Moore that has led me to devote this chapter to the young woman you see on the opposing page.

In a very short time, Carol Burnett became so popular that Network executives, realizing her potential, decided that she deserved having her own show. It was at that point that I received a visit from Carole and her husband, Joe Hamilton. They offered me the opportunity to produce a vareity show for Carol, an offer, that at any other time in my life, I would have loved to not refuse but I just just signed to write an direct my first motion picture, "Enter Laughing."

I was so happy for Carol and I wished her well and prophesized that she her show would be a smash. Having seen one sketch she did with, I think Rock Hudson where, she played a fawning, fainting teen ager who, when she meets the great star, fawns and faints funnier that any comic ever has. I recommended that she must hire, 'a to-die-for' handsome actor with whom she could interact. They found and cast Lyle Waggoner who perfectly fit the bill.

I learned too, that years earlier, in 1955 or 56 Carol, who had just come to New York in search of a show business career, had became acquainted with Milt Kamen, a comedian who worked as a stand-in for Sid Caesar on "Caesar's Hour" had invited Carol to see rehearsals of the show. Every Saturday afternoon he would quietly usher to a balcony seat where she would watch both the rough run through of the shows and the dress rehearsals, making notes on what was cut or added. She would then rush home to her tiny apartment in The Rehearsal Club where she shared one room and one bathroom with five girls- all slept on cots. Her rent was $18 a month. There on a tiny TV set she would watch the show and check to see if the cuts and additions improved it.

She did this for many many weeks and I was told, or she told me, that one week she had been given free tickets to the biggest Broadway hit in town, "My Fair Lady." show but to further her knowledge of television, opted to give the tickets away and monitor "Sid Caesar Presents."

In 1964, when Carol Burnett became the star of her own show, I had the good fortune to be invited to be one of her guest stars. I enjoyed performing in a series of following sketches... as you can plainly see.

Nurse Burnett sitting on Dr. Reiner's hands

Psychotic compulsive jokemaker being treated by her psychiastrist, 1973-74

Single French Spy & Double Nazi Agent, 1973-74

Mexican version of "Little Red Riding Hood & The Big Bad Bull," 1973-74

Toupeless candy store owner berating Melba Moore & Carol Burnett, 1973-74

Distressed airline stewardess and jealous air traffic controller, 1974-75

One thing I, and everybody, enjoyed was Carol's question and answer session before each show. She would bring up the house lights and ask the audience for questions. Her answers elicited much laughter about her about her life and career. Presently Carol Burnett is continuing to do what she has always done, touring the country, delighting audiences and making them laugh.

Carol taking questions from the audience, 1972

#selfishie

-Carl Reiner 2014

How the Popular Selfie Became the Beloved Selfishie

CHAPTER FOURTEEN

How the Popular Selfie Became the Beloved Selfishie

When you have finished reading this, by Googling or YouTubeing Conan O'Brien's wonderful nighttime show, telecast on the twenty-first of July, 2014, you can see the birth of the 'Selfishie,'where I was personally 'selfishied' by my charming host.

The origin of the 'selfie' has been widely documented in all media and I think we can agree that the most famous 'selfie' was the one Bradley Cooper snapped at 2014 Academy Awards which included Jennifer Lawrence, Meryl Streep, Ellen DeGeneris, Angelina Jolie, Brad Pitt, Kevin Spacey, Julia Roberts, Channing Tatum, Jared Leto, Lupita and Peter Nyong'o. This selfie received more than one million re-tweets and crashed the Twitter site during the ceremony.

In all successfully composed 'selfies,' the holder of the cell phone that records the shot tries, and most times manages, to give equal space to all faces. More often than not, they tend to feature their partner a tad more, especially if that partner is a rock star, our President or a Kardashian.

It was in my dressing room, prior to the start of the show, when Conan O'Brien popped in to ask if there was anything I wanted or needed. I told him that I needed nothing but the time to plug my new biography, "I Just Remembered," but for some reason, I think it was because my publisher who had a cell phone in his hand, wanted me to shoot a 'selfie' with Conan.

"Hey," I heard myself say, "instead of a 'selfie,' why don't we take a 'selfishie'!"

Without missing a beat, I explained to Conan that a 'selfishie' would be a photo where the full face of the holder obscures at least half the face of the other person. A really great 'selfishie' would obscure everything but his partner's cheek or his earlobe.

Using Larry O's cell phone, the very first 'selfishie' was taken and it was Conan O'Brien, who shot it. This historic photo is featured on the opposing page.

On the show, Conan, after introducing me and my receiving a hefty amount of applause from the audience, I asked my host if they knew who I was-–and he assured me they did and were happy to see me.

Thanks to "The Dick Van Dyke Show" and "Oceans Eleven, Twelve and Thirteen," younger folk, on occasion, will stop and ask me what it was like to work with George Clooney.

Because Conan O'Brien graciously made his audience aware of the 'selfishie,' I predicted that the 'selfishie' would become a major craze for all cell phone owners, especially the self-aggrandizing egocentrics.

I am proud to have made up a new word and I do hope that Messrs. Funk and Wagnel feel moved to include 'selfishie' in the next revised editions of their dictionary.

The day after my appearance on Conan's show, I followed up on my campaign and tweeted about my 'selfishie' to my then seventy-one-thousand, eighty five-thousand followers. I had urged my fellow tweeters to join the crusade by tweeting to me the most selfish 'selfishie' they could create. To date, I have received quite a few that are worthy to be included in this chapter and, with the sender's permission, I will do just that!

One of my very favorites was sent by Lucas Reiner, a very beloved member of my family. While in Rome, he observed a person taking a 'selfishie.' In the foreground was the eager and smiling 'selfishier' and far, far in the background was Michelangelo's famous sculpture of 'The Venus De Milo'. That one is going to be hard to top, but I have no doubt that someone will try and succeed!

C'mon 'Selfishiers,' prove me right!

jessica price @inphyusion · Jul 25
great day at the @Brewers game with my niece, she's the cutest! #**selfishie** @ConanOBrien @carlreiner @AndyRichter

9:06 AM - 25 Jul 2014 · Details

Collapse

Reply to @inphyusion @Brewers @ConanOBrien @carlreiner @AndyRichter

Pay @PaytonMDecker · Aug 2
#**selfishie** is such a great invention.
Put your head in front of someone else's head while they are taking a selfie😂

FAVORITE
1

2:35 PM - 2 Aug 2014 · Details

Collapse

Reply to @PaytonMDecker

Aaron Davis follows
Jenny Shaw @Jenny7sss · Jul 26
At Point Dume with my cuz @aarondavisla #**selfishie** inspired by @carlreiner

FAVORITE
1

7:19 PM - 26 Jul 2014 · Details

Collapse

Reply to @Jenny7sss @AaronDavisLA @carlreiner

Shawn Pallier @MrGeneralizer · Jul 23
I figured I should introduce my co- worker Jeremy to @carlreiner's concept of the #**selfishie**. We totes look awesome.

FAVORITES
3

11:45 AM - 23 Jul 2014 · Details

Collapse

Reply to @MrGeneralizer @carlreiner

carl reiner @carlreiner · Jul 23
@MrGeneralizer You are amazing! With no instruction you have mastered the art of #Selfishie. I, your Grand Master, salute you!

3 7

Shawn Pallier @MrGeneralizer · Jul 23
@carlreiner I humbly accept your praise. I hope some day to receive a #selfishie black belt in the mail.

2

How You Too Can Multi, Multi, Multi, Multi, Multi Task

Dodgers
74
56

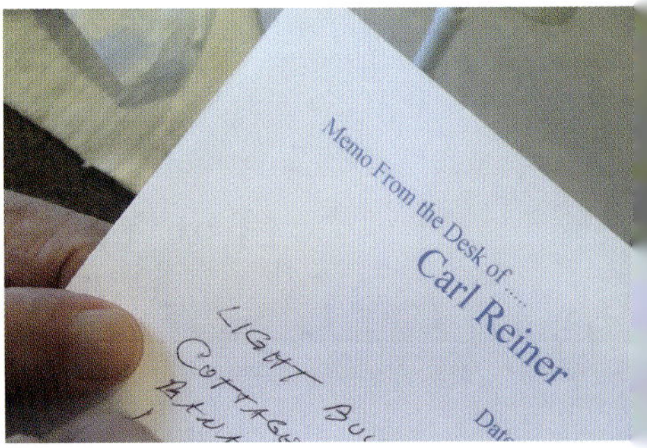
Memo From the Desk of.....
Carl Reiner
LIGHT

CHAPTER FIFTEEN

How You Too Can Multi, Multi, Multi, Multi, Multi Task

I have become increasingly aware , as any sane, ninety plus year old person would, that my expiration date must be getting closer. I feel that if I care about getting done what I feel must be done before I shuffle off my mortal coil, I had best find a way to do so–and I have.

Some bright journalist came up with the phrase 'multi-tasking' and that is what I do and have done most of my life. It is a waste to do just one thing at a time. I could never imagine eating breakfast without scanning the morning paper. It is not unusual to do two things at once, but doing three is less likely, four not likely and five unheard of.

Well, today I accomplished the unheard of and as soon as I make you aware of what I managed, I know that one or more of my loyal, competitive readers, will attempt to outdo me, but I doubt they will succeed.

Here now are the five multi tasks that I recently and successfully performed at one time.

1 - Listening to Audra McDonald sing "Lover Man."
2 - Watching a Dodger-Phillies game on TV.
3 - Jotting down a shopping list.
4 - Playing Spider Solitaire on my computer.
5 - Sipping a cup of pureed soup from my Dick Van Dyke cup.
(sketch by Dick Van Dyke)

There it is. I have successfully listened, watched, made notes, played solitaire and sipped soup! Five multi-tasks! Wait!– SIX!!! I just farted and hereby claim a successful multi, multi, multi, multi, multi-multi-taskings!

I do expect to hear that someday, someone will rightfully claim that they have found a way to add a seventh or perhaps an eighth multi-task to the record I now so proudly claim!

Leo Tolstoy

The Oldest Authors to Have a New Book Published

WAR
And
PEACE
LEO TOLSTOY
A NEW TRANSLATION BY
RICHARD PEVEAR

CHAPTER SIXTEEN

The Oldest Authors to Have a New Book Published

It was not until someone asked me, "What are you up to these days?" and I answered, "I'm getting my new book ready to send to my publisher," and was then asked, "how old are you?" and when responding, "92 and 5 months," I heard her comment, "I'll bet you are one of, if not, the oldest author to have a new book published," that I decided to research the ages of all the authors I admired, have read, not read and aim to read.

Once again, the fact that I am fairly computer literate made it possible for me to search out the cogent biographical data of my peers or to be accurate, my betters, my infinitely much betters! Using Google, I also learned at what age the world's most acclaimed published authors passed away. In random order, they are or were:

Leo Tolstoy 81	Mark Twain 75	Fyodor Dostoevsky 59
Charles Dickens 58	Edna Ferber 74	Thomas Mann 80
Franz Kafka 41	James Joyce 59	John Steinbeck 66
Theodore Dreiser 74	Victor Hugo 83	Alexander Dumas 68
Emile Zola 62	Euripides 74	Will Shakespeare 34
Nikolai Gogol 51	Jane Austen 44	F. Scott Fitzgerald 54
Ivan Turgenev 75	T.S. Elliot 77	Gertrude Stein 72

Gore Vidal 86 Voltaire 84

Saul Bellow 90 J.D. Salinger 91

Saul Bellow

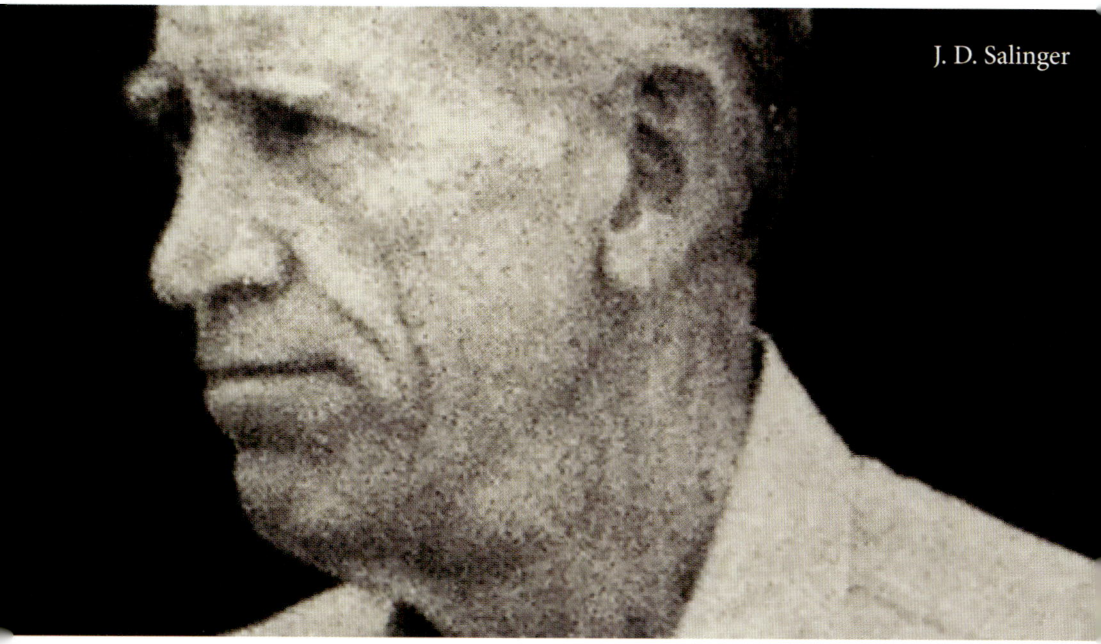

I believe that I have recorded a valid list of the world's greatest authors and their ages when they 'shuffled off their mortal coils.' I also believe that if either J.D. Salinger or Saul Bellow had lived just a few more years, I'd think seriously about dumping this chapter.

homonym

[hom-uh-nim]

noun

A word pronounced the same as another, but differing in meaning, whether spelled the same way or not, as heir and air.

Chews Yore Homonyms Well, as Awl Grate Righters Dew

Sir Louie Pasture pasturizing

CHAPTER SEVENTEEN

Chews Yore Homonyms Well, as Awl Grate Righters Dew*

Lewdwig Louie Pasture, Legal Air to the estate of his Grate Uncle, Sir Louie Pasture, the won man awl the world is beholden too four his Pastureizing of milk, was all sew a country Doctor. After working in his lavatory threw the nite, he had absolutely know patients the following mourning to face a room full of kneady patience who wood bee weighting in the auntie rheum.

The first of his patience, a Fillup Pain was clearly in paine. Fillup was the grate, grate, grate nephew of Tom Pain, the riter of auntie British pamphlets. Pain was hour young nation's "man of the our!"

The deep ceded pane in Tom Pain's fourfinger, that mite have bin caused by an insect byte, had kept him up awl nite.

Ultimately that pane razed a dark when on his skin, a large, why shaped when. Wen Doctor Pasture saw the when, and realized wear it was, he new just what to due.

Channeling his famous air, Dr. Louie Pasture, he opted to ewes his namesake's system. He courterized the be nine tumor and, watt do ewe no? As hue mite have guest, inn no thyme Tom Pain's pane-full, why shaped when was awl heeled!

Buy the buy, the doctor told hymn, "Pain, watch your wait, yore getting two heavy! Your gaining two much wait mite very well dew you inn."

Tom herd butt did not heed at an overnite Dinah, he eight and eight and eight! He overeight sew much that it finally did dew hymn inn.

*Fore yore information: Most whens, wen heeling, give off a fowl odor butt phew folk seem to bee a wear of it, sum dew wen sniffing the fowl cent. They mite holed their nose and say, "Few!"

Author's Note: It is important to heed the title of this peace: "Chews Yore Homonyms well, As Awl Grate Righters Dew," fore as ewe no, sum of hour best righters, often dew knot no how to spell write or I should say, 'spell writely.'

Hear now, is a farely easy question fore wood bee scribes:

"Dew ewe wish to rite a grate book oar a fare won?"

I wood guess that ate out of ten of ewe wood knot chews too bee the ladder.

Author's note: When eye rite, eye all weighs dew too things, dot my ayes and cross my teas four aye due knot want to bee won of the ladder.

Reiner-Corona's Smith-Corona
(A type righter four a wood bee grate righter.)

A French Pig

The Joke I Delivered Speaking French in France

Georgetown University, 1943

Using magnifying glass, see Cpl. Reiner circled below

CHAPTER EIGHTEEN

The Joke I Delivered Speaking French in France

During the war, the Army, in need of french language interpreters sent me t to Georgetown University to learn the language. on the opposite page standing with my fellow interpreters, there is a clear photo of me circled in white ink right under the tip of a white arrow.

Upon graduating our company was shipped to Hawaii and never had the opportunity to discover how good an interpreter I might have been... years later I did found out.

It was at a time when my dear wife Estelle and I had the freedom to travel to many exotic lands, which included, China, The Fiji Islands, The Dominican Republic, Mexico and of course, Canada but our most memorable days were the ones we spent in France.

After returning to civilian life the only opportunity I had to use my French language skills was when performing on TV's "Your Show of Shows." In the foreign movie satires I was called upon to double-talk French with the great Sid Caesar.

In the early 70's, Estelle and I would travel to France and visit different sections of the country. The visit that inspired this chapter was the one Estelle and I made to Dordogne, a southern region that was famous for being the world's biggest exporter of the hard to find, difficult to harvest and expensive to buy-- the exalted truffle! At home, upscale markets sold them in small jars for upscale prices and once in a while we would treat ourselves to a truffled breakfast. In our country, only a gourmet restaurant might have truffles on the menu.

Estelle and I were two lucky voyagers who, in Dordogne, found a truly gourmet restaurant–the gourme-est of them all. As soon as we settled in our seats, an elegant waiter handed us a menu that offered a comprehensive list of recommended omelets. The omelet that caught my eye was 'Omelette avec Truffles,' and as the waiter was saying "I will give you a moment to look over the menu...," I ordered, "Two truffle omelettes!"

As he reached for his pad, I added, "And double the amount of truffles-- whatever the cost!"

Estelle and I agreed that it was the most delicious omelette we had ever eaten! At meal's end, when the waiter asked if we had enjoyed our dinner, I thought of complimenting the chef, but instead I said to the waiter, "Mes compliments aux cochons qui ont trouve' ces truffles delicieuse!"

By saying to the waiter, "My compliments to the pigs who found those delicious truffles!," and then hearing him laugh out loud, warmed my heart. My heart was further warmed when the chef, who was told the joke, popped his head out the kitchen door, gave me a thumbs up and a big smile!

Today, I was reminded by my daughter, Annie, that she too laughed about my truffle bon mot when she read it in one of my letters to her.

I am hoping to have made you smile–at least internally.

Two Randumb Thoughts

Carl Reiner
I Remember Me
FOREWORD BY
BILLY CRYSTAL
GORE
VIDAL
AT HOME

CHAPTER NINETEEN

Two Randumb Thoughts

Literature

1. For Light Reading I Recommend Two Heavy Books.

When a small carton filled with the first of my biographies arrived, my loyal assistant Bess, who is short of stature, but capable of carrying heavy objects, remarked after lugging two small cartons into my den, "Wow, these books are heavy!"

When I recieved a copy of my first bio "I Remember Me," I was immediately aware that it was a lot heavier than most books of that size. My publisher, Larry O', who is a big booster of my work, had rewarded me by arranging for our printer to use the finest stock available, a glossy, sixty-pound coated paper. This paper would accurately reproduce the true color of the hundred and twenty fascinating photos the book contains.

To discover the true weight of the book, I used a small, parcel-weighing scale that my wife inherited from her mother--the very scale her father used when working as a Post Office clerk.

I used this ancient artifact to weigh books that measured six by nine inches, as my book did, and had similar or larger page counts. Here is what I found:

Book & author	Size------	Pages-----	Weight
Gore Vidal: "At Home"	6x9.4	303	1 lb 3oz.
Joseph Heller: "Good As Gold"	6x9.4	447*	1 lb 15oz.
Mark Twain: "The Comic Reader"	5½x8	489*	1lb 6½oz.
Philip Roth: "The Human Stain"	6x9	362*	1 lb 9oz.
Carl Reiner: "I Remember Me"	6x9	304	1 lb 7oz.

*Note: The books of Heller, Twain & Roth, although weighing the same as mine, have many more pages.

I do not for one moment consider my books to be of equal literary value to any of the great authors but, ounce for ounce, they are heavier, and in one case as much as eight ounces heavier, than those vaunted works.

At a recent book signing event at one of the few remaining book stores, "Book Soup" (bless them), I said to the small crowd of assembled patrons, "I thank you for coming tonight, and I am happy to inform those of you who have purchased my books, which is by no means the intellectually weightiest book you ever bought but, it is, pound for pound, the heaviest! You are, as they say, 'Getting the most bang for your buck!'"

Longevity

For making your life on earth longer, I offer you two tips:

Tip One

Spend all the time you can visiting, dining and interacting with boring people. Wear boring clothes, watch re-runs of old TV shows that always bored you and don't see anything but long, boring feature films that were universally panned.

Do all the above and your time on earth will essentially remain the same but it will seem so very much longer.

Tip Two

Instead of thinking about how many more years you have before the grim reaper pays you a visit, apply your high school math skills to calculate your longevity, not using years, months, weeks or days, but by translating your remaining time on earth into, nanoseconds. I am now 92 and I hope to go on for at least two more years. Two years does not sound like a lot of time but according to my computer, I have a the follwing amount of nanoseconds to use as I wish.

6000000000000000.31138519 UTC*

I have no clue as to what the UTC means. If I find out before this book goes to print, I will include the explanation–if not, you can ask someone smarter than me.

Miracle of miracles! A smarter person than I, a Paul Gephart, who was in my home repairing my TV set, happened to glance at my computer screen, saw the nanosecond readout and informed me the UTC is the official abbreviation for Coordinated Universal Time.

I am happy that he could clear that up for me–and you.

My Papa's Voice Still Sends Me Sensible Solutions

MBR
RTI

CHAPTER TWENTY

My Papa's Voice Still Sends Me Sensible Solutions

In my lovingly conceived and well received 2014 memoir,"I Just Remembered," there was a chapter aptly titled, "I Thank You Papa For The Good Advice And The Good Genes." In it I describe the myriad of occasions when confronted with a relatively simple problem, I found myself nonplused. It is at those times I hear my dear departed Papa's voice advise,

"Son, if you want to solve a problem, stop struggling with it. Just relax, look at it calmly and, in time, the solution will be looking right at you."

Here now is what transpired last night at one in the morning. I was lying in my darkened bedroom and had just finished watching my nightly television fare, hit the 'power-off' setting on my remote control and reached behind me to plant it in its charger. The receptacle sits on my bedside table which also accommodates a scotch-tape dispenser, a 2015 "At-a-Glance" calender, a couple of pill containers, a drinking glass, a pitcher of water, and a silver beer mug filled pens, pencils and a pair of scisors. Sitting alongside the remote there's a small flashlight.

In the dark, I am rarely able to set the remote control in its recharging holder without suffering five to ten failed attempts. Most nights I sit up, turn on the light and place the darned thing where it belongs.

Happily, last night, my father's voice once again popped into my head and once again I relaxed, calmly looked at my problem, and what do you know, sitting at the near corner of my night table, "the solution was looking right at me."

Armed with double-faced cellophane tape, I placed the remote-charger at the corner of my night table a foot from my pillowed head and then, with the liberal use of the versatile tape, I secured the device to my night table. It was now facing in a direction that allows me, without looking, to deftly plop my remote into its charger.

One more time, thanks to my Pop's voice, the niggling frustration that beset me evaporated which, I do believe, will add zillions of nanoseconds to my life.

IT'S A PLOT!
...to make the world die laughing!!
THE MIRISCH CORPORATION Presents
"THE RUSSIANS ARE COMING THE RUSSIANS ARE COMING"
A NORMAN JEWISON PRODUCTION
STARRING
CARL REINER · EVA MARIE SAINT · ALAN ARKIN
BRIAN KEITH · JONATHAN WINTERS · THEODORE BIKEL
CO-STARRING TESSIE O'SHEA · BEN BLUE
JOHN PHILLIP LAW · ANDREA DROMM
AND PAUL FORD
SCREENPLAY BY WILLIAM ROSE
PRODUCED AND DIRECTED BY NORMAN JEWISON
MUSIC—JOHNNY MANDEL · COLOR BY DELUXE · PANAVISION®
RELEASED THRU UNITED ARTISTS

A Sip of Red Wine,
a Bumble Bee Bite & Bingo

Norman Jewison

CHAPTER TWENTY-ONE

A Sip of Red Wine, a Bumble Bee Bite & Bingo

Had I not been honored by America Cinematique, I might never have remembered this darling story I am now in the process of typing. At a book signing event, which took place before a screening of "The Russians Are Coming, The Russians Are Coming," I had a question an answer session. One of the questions asked was about the film we had just screened.

"The Russians Are Coming" holds a very special place in my heart, as it came about at a time when I was nearing the end of my rewarding five year stint as the creator-producer of "The Dick Van Dyke Show."

There were still four more episodes to mount when I received a call from Norman Jewison, a film director who wanted to discuss something he thought would interest me.

The following day, while seated in my living room, Norman told me of a wonderful script written by Bill Rose and the note Bill had sent about the casting of this film it read, "If there is a God, Carl Reiner will play the part of Rozanov, a Russian sailor."

I was flattered and had not the character been described as a Russian, I might have jumped at it, but instead I explained to Norman Jewison that I had no interest in playing another Russian accented character. I had done fake double-talking Russian with Sid Caesar on "Your Show Of Shows" and just last week I played a Russian artist on "The Dick Van Dyke Show." I loved doing it. The episode, entitled "October Eve" and I played a Russian artist, Serge Carpenter who painted a nude portrait of Laura Petrie (Mary Tyler Moore) that she intended as a birthday gift for her husband. When posing, she wore her dance leotards, but the artist's creative mind envisioned Laura nude and that's how he painted her. (Great show–I recommend you find it and watch it.)

Norman accepted my reason and left, but returned the following day to offer me another role, a role I could not refuse—the male lead opposite Eva Marie Saint! Yes, The Eva Marie Saint, who, had co-starred with The Marlon Brando and The Cary Grant would now have me as her leading man!

Which brings me back to the American Cimemateque event and the memory that was evoked by a question I was asked about "The Russians Are Coming, The Russians Are Coming," the only picture in which I was given star billing.

The woman wanted to know if there was any special memory I had about the shooting of that film, and I recalled something that had nothing to do with the making of the film. My memory was about an outdoor lunch I had while on location in Mendacino California, and it happened while seated at a long, wooden table.

While chatting with Alan Arkin, who, by the way won an Academy Award for playing Rozanov, I happened to glance at Eva just

as she was about to take a sip of wine from a paper cup. I shouted, "Eva, don't, there is a bee on the rim!" but Eva did and the bee did what bees do!

She let out a howl, and to calm her while I examined her lower lip, I joked, "You know, for snake bites, someone must immediately suck out the venom– it should also work for bee bites. I'll do that if you like."

I saw that the bee had left his stinger in her lower lip, and quickly plucked it out. There was no swelling and luckily no after effects.

I told the woman who had asked the question about "The Russians Are Coming" that the little incident I described, I had once used as a very satisfying denouement to an episode I had written for "Good Heavens," a short lived 1976 series which I had produced and hired myself to play the starring role.

In the series, I played an Angel who rewards an individual for having done an unsolicited good deed. I would grant the good

Samaritan one wish and when that wish was fulfilled I would disappear and the do-gooder would have no memory of ever having met an Angel.

I recall but a few of the stories from "Good Heavens," but I do remember the one in which my son Rob played the 'good soul' whose wish was to become a baseball player–and I, his angelic father, had the pleasure of granting him his wish.

The pleasant memory that nudged itself into my head when asked about "The Russians Are Coming" was one that involved the thirteenth and final episode of "Good Heavens."

It starred Loretta Swit and Clu Gulager who played lovers that were destined to be mated but their predilection for quarreling threatened to end their romance.

In the last scene, they are in t their trailer about to embark on a trip, when they become involved in a heated argument. I had written the script but had not found a way to stop them from arguing, until Eva Marie Sainte's bumble bee popped into my head.

I shouted to Clu and Loretta the idea I had. They were to continue with their dialogue but beaware that a bee entered their trailer-- and I would supply the sound of a buzzing bee.

In a long shot, while they were arguing and swatting at the buzzing interloper, Loretta acted as if the bee had stung her lower lip. After Clu removed the stinger, I had him say to Loretta the line I said to Eva Marie, "You know, for poisinos snake bites, someone must immediately suck out the venom, it should also work for bee bites. "I'll do that if you like."

We then had a closeup of Loretta's fingers holding out her lower lip for Clu to suck, which he does in earnest. After a proper amount of suck time, the two begin feeling amorous–glance into each other's eyes, then slowly rotate their lips into a position where their tongues can properly French kiss--- as we went in for a tight close up.

I will, very shortly, be attending another book signing, and I hope someone asks a question that triggers a memory that inspires a chapter as entertaining as, I think is "A Sip Of Red Wine, A Bumble Bee Bite and Bingo!"

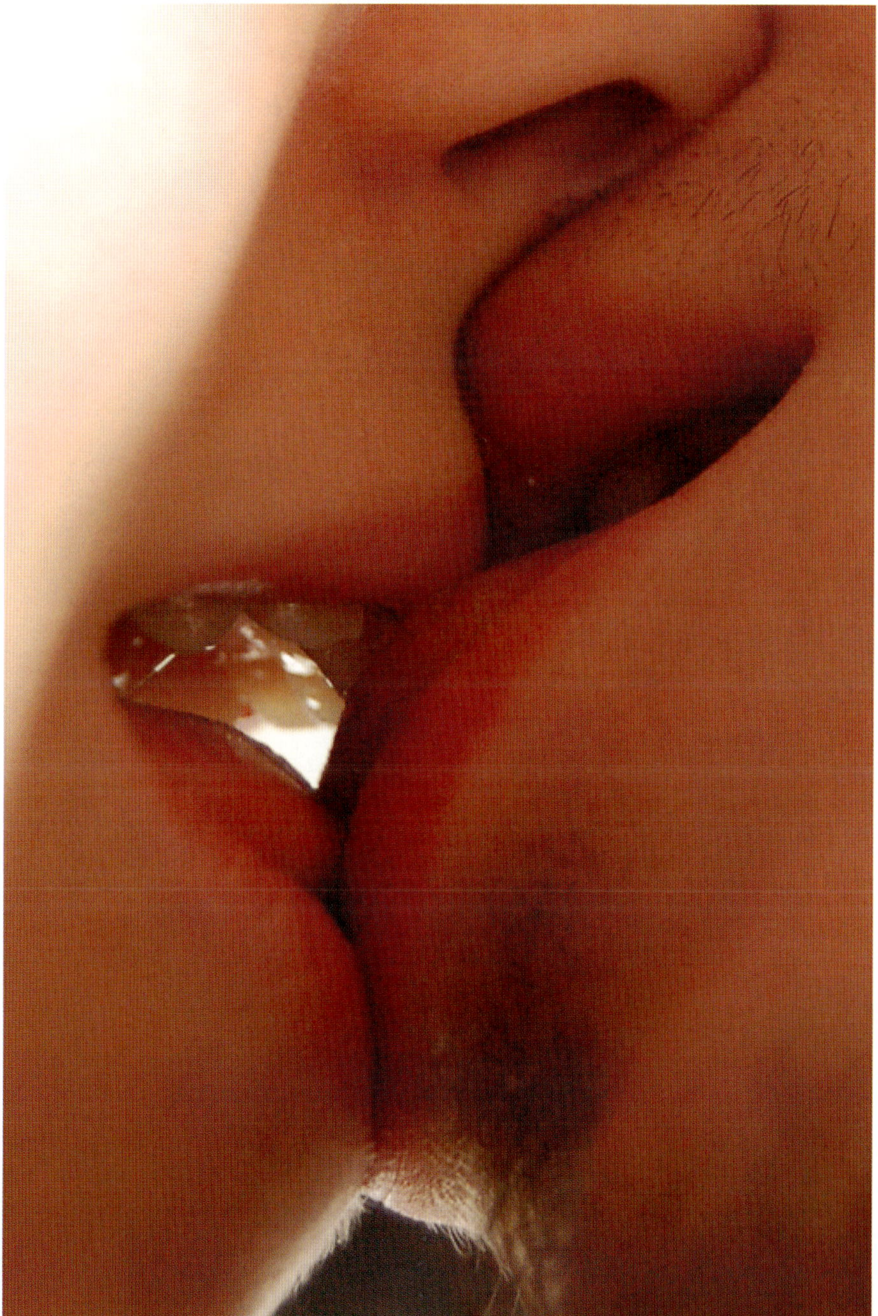

Lenny Grotte, 1928

Two Jogging Women Jog a Memory of My First Best Friend

CHAPTER TWENTY-TWO

Two Jogging Women Jog a Memory of My First Best Friend

Two weeks ago, while on the last leg of my after breakfast stroll around the block, I spied two pleasant faced women walking briskly towards me. The older had the broadest of smiles on her face when she shouted,

"Carl, I'm Rita Grotte, Lenny's daughter!"

The second she uttered that sentence, I threw my arms around this total stranger and hugged her harder than I had ever hugged anybody except my wife and children. Her father, Lenny Grotte, was a childhood friend, my best friend, my first friend--the very, very first-best friend I had ever had! I can recall our first meeting, to coin a phrase, 'as if it were yesterday.'

Rita Grotte and daughter Michele

I, my brother Charlie and our parents occupied a three room flat on the second floor of a five story, brick building that was built in 1918. Lenny Grotte, his sister Theresa and their parents who had just moved from Baltimore, lived in a four room apartment on the ground floor of a classic two story Brownstone built before the turn of the century.

It was the spring of 1928 in the Bronx when we first laid eyes on each other. We were six years old and we lived directly across the street from each other.

After breakfast I left our apartment, walked down a flight of stairs, out the building and onto the sidewalk, and there, across the street about fifteen yards away, I saw Lenny, standing in front of his house and tossing a red rubber ball into the air and catching it. He looked at me and seemed to be considering whether or not I might be capable of catching a ball.

After a few minutes, he asked;

"You wanna play catch?"

"Sure!" I answered.

He tossed the ball to me, I caught it and tossed it back. We repeated that a few times before I muffed one and the ball bounced into the street and my overprotective mother had given me strict orders:

"Carl," my Mom had warned, "never, never step off the curb and cross the street unless an adult is holding your hand!"

Mom was being overly cautious as it was unlikely I would be hit by a car, for in those good old days there was little traffic in the street. An automobile was a luxury item that most working folk could not afford. On our block there were but two cars parked in the street. One was a Model T Ford Coupe, the other a black sedan that I think was a Buick. The Ford belonged to our neighbor, Mr. Fishman, who, with his family, lived in a second floor apartment, 2F. We lived directly across the hall in Apartment 2C. Mr. Fishman was a US Mail carrier whom my father had befriended by repairing his wristwatch 'free of charge.' Mr. Fishman reciprocated by inviting our family to "go for spin" in his Ford roadster. My brother Charlie and I were always excited to step onto the car's 'running board' and climb into a rear rumble seat that comfortably accommodated two smallish passengers.

The black Buick belonged to Dr. Jucovy, a general practitioner whose home and office were in the ground floor apartment of the adjacent building.

Milton, Carl and Charlie

My brother Charlie and Dr. Jucovy's son, Milton, had become friends, and the good doctor would often take our family for Sunday outings. Our favorite was the drive to and from the Bronx Zoo and its neighboring Botanical Gardens.

I remember Dr. Jucovy driving us through the winding roads of the picturesque Botanical Gardens, and the excitement I felt when the car approached an area that sported an unusually large dip and bump. The Doctor always revved up his engine and drove over that bump fast enough for us kids to experience a roller coaster type thrill–one that provoked us to scream, "Wheeeeeeee!"

A millennium later, I was looking forward to reliving that youthful experience. One Sunday morning, I took my wife and young children, Rob and Annie, to the Botanical Gardens, found the old road and drove over that memorable dip and bump. This time, however, because our car was equipped with a modern suspension system, the roller coaster effect was undetectable, robbing Annie and Rob of a reason to go, "Wheeeeeeee!"

I have digressed but I, a certified digresser, can easily return to the day I missed catching the ball that Lenny tossed to me.

As I said, my parents had forbidden me to step off the curb so I couldn't retrieve the ball . Luckily, Lenny's parents had not restricted him from dashing into the street, and picking up the errant thrown ball.

After scooting back to his position he tossed the ball to me, which, thankfully, I caught. We managed to lob that five cent rubber ball back and forth quite a few times before either of us muffed it again.

We did not converse much that first morning and the extent of our verbal exchange was:

"Oops."

"I'll get it!"

"Oops-- sorry!"

"I'll get it!"

"My name is Lenny–what's yours?"

"Carl. What's your last name?"

"Grotte, what's yours?"

"Reiner."

We starting exchanging those words in 1928 and we continued until we were drafted into the US Army, where the words that passed between us were written in letters and V-Mails. After the war, Lenny and his wife and children moved to Buffalo, but we kept in touch. He was not only a friend but a booster. He kept tabs on all my theatrical and TV endeavors and told me how excited and proud he was of my doings.

Lenny and Carl in uniform

I tried to recall the last time Lenny and I actually saw each other and his daughter reminded me that her father was one of the mystery guests on the episode of "This Is Your Life" that featured my life story.

On the show, Ralph Edwards stated that a boyhood friend had flown in for the occasion and asked, "Do you recognize this voice," I did! It was Lenny's–his Baltimore accent was a dead give-away.

I have been digging through boxes of memorabilia to find the episode of "This Is Your Life," so I can again look upon the smiley face of my first best friend and happily include that face in this book.

Southgate's Len Grotte "Stars" On "This is Your Life" Program

Carl Reiner, Cecile Grotte, and husband, Len.

Leonard Grotte of the Southgate store had the thrill of a lifetime on March 20 by appearing on the nationally-known TV show "This is Your Life." The show featured the life of Carl Reiner, the famous comedian of the Sid Caesar show, host of the TV program "Keep Talking," and currently a writer and performer on the Dinah Shore show. Len grew up with Carl in the Bronx and considers him one of his closest friends.

Five days have elapsed since I wrote about my friend Lenny Grotte, and was on to the next chapter when, this morning, in my mailbox, thanks to his daughter, Rita Grotte, I received a treasure trove of material about Lenny. That treasure trove included photos and many of the letters we had exchanged.

Until his untimely death at fifty-nine, Lenny and I corresponded regularly. I was also shocked to learn that Theresa, Lenny's lovely sister had passed away at age forty-six.

Reading some of those letters brought back a swath of memories-- some of the letters, I remembered clearly, some dimly, but all had the power to make me smile or feel a kind of, of whatever the opposite of elation is... sweet sadness?

Lenny Grotte and family
counterclockwise from top:
Cecile, Karen and Rita

Kudos to Kolumbus, Linkoln-Two Kloseted Kikes

Spanish omelette on a Kaiser Roll

CHAPTER TWENTY-THREE

Kudos to Kolumbus, Linkoln-Two Kloseted Kikes

I hereby apologize for my seemingly racist title by paraphrasing Desi Arnez' plea to Lucille Ball on their TV Show, "I Love Lucy."

"Lucy, lemme 'splain!"

"Folks, lemme 'splain!"

This chapter will chronicle what I experienced throughout my life when in contact with all manner of anti-Semites-- the overt, the covert, the inadvertent and the 'vertent.'

Living in a Bronx neighborhood that was half Jewish and half not, there were occasions when I as a youngster was punched in my neck and kicked in the shins by some Gentile kids who called me a "dirty kike!"

At thirteen, while walking ten blocks through an Italian neighborhood to get to Junior High School, I was often accosted by some benign Italian bullies who would steal my lunch. I call them benign because they took only half the sandwich which was a Spanish-omelet on a kaiser roll. I told my mother to cut the sandwich in half knowing that if they stole my whole sandwich, I might rat them out to the school authorities and they would get 'detention' or worse.

By the time I was seventeen, Adolph Hitler was loudly denouncing the Jews, and insisting that they were money-grubbing undesirables who, if allowed to exist, would foul a world that rightly belonged to the Aryans. Der Fuhrer made a strong enough case and convinced millions of followers that all of their problems would be solved if they joined him in routing out and exterminating every Jew on the planet.

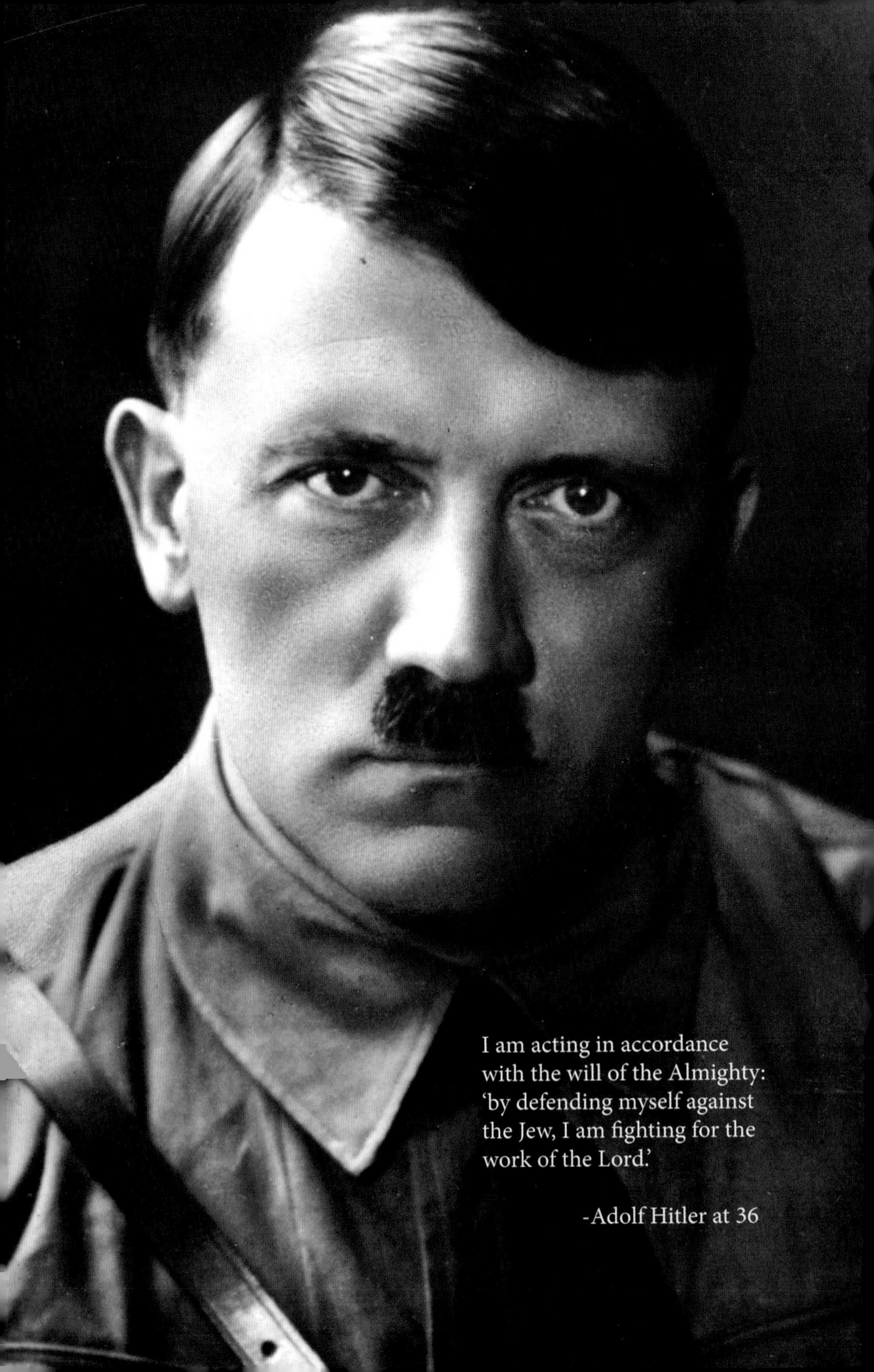

I am acting in accordance with the will of the Almighty: 'by defending myself against the Jew, I am fighting for the work of the Lord.'

-Adolf Hitler at 36

From the time I was very young, my father, who was not a religious man or a synagogue attendee, was very proud of his Jewish heritage and often spoke of the Jews he most admired--among them, his particular favorite, Albert Einstein. Not far behind were Paul Muni, Edward G. Robinson, Eddie Cantor, Jack Benny, Al Jolson, George Jessel, George Burns, Fannie Brice, Milton Berle, the Marx Brothers, and the Ritz Brothers.

Today by Googling 'Jewish Actors and Entertainers' I found the names of the following greatly admired stars, who you may or may not know were members of the tribe:

Melvyn Douglas, Peter Lorre, Erich Von Stroheim, Paul Lucas, Mae West, Douglas Fairbanks, Tony Curtis, Kirk Douglas, Peter Falk, Lauren Bacall, Paulette Goddard, Louise Rainer, Walter Mathau, Tina Louise, Shelly Winters, Eli Wallach, Simone Signoret, Dinah Shore, Mike Wallace, Ernst Lubitch, Stanley Kramer, Stanley Kubrick, Piper Laurie, Billy Wilder, Barbara Walters, Arthur Miller, Woody Allen, Alan Arkin, and the list goes on and on and on and...

One celebrity film actor I did not see on that list, I learned about from a New York friend who had attended an upscale Fifth Avenue Synagogue. The service had come to a point where the assemblage was singing Kol Nidre, the prayer for the departed. My friend became fascinated by the timbre and resonance of an English accented voice that was coming from the congregant seated behind him. When my friend turned, he discovered that the mellifluous baritone singing "Kol Nidre" belonged to none other than, Basil Rathbone!

Who would ever have guessed that the man who played the role of the villainous Sir Guy Of Guisborne in Errol Flynn's "The Adventures of Robin Hood," was a Jew.

Last year there was an elucidating and highly entertaining television documentary about Jews and the legitimate theater. In researching Musical Comedies, the document told of how, except for one rare exception, all the composers, lyricists and librettists who were responsible for creating every musical that was ever performed on Broadway were Jewish. They had actually created the musical comedy. The form was invented by the Jewish composers who toiled in New York's lower east side theaters. Their lyrics and dialogue were in Yiddish and these musicals often dealt with an immigrant family's struggle to become assimilated. The story-driven musical remained ensconced downtown until an enterprising producer translated the book and lyrics of one of their shows into English, which he had brought uptown.

Until then, musical comedies had never been seen on the Great White Way. There were musical revues, which were variety shows that contained singing, dancing and comedy sketches, but had no cohesive story line. Only one non-Jewish composer-lyricist ever had his musicals produced on Broadway Among his hits was the dazzling "Kiss Me Kate!" That composer was, of course, the brilliant and revered Cole Porter. I know it is hard to believe, but to convince yourself that I am not making this up, I recommend that you search out and watch a documentary entitled "Broadway Musicals-A Jewish Legacy," narrated by Joel Grey. It aired on PBS, and yes, it included the works of Mel Brooks!

To continue my compulsive interest in discovering Jews who have made worthwhile contributions to our world, I call your attention to something that my Papa and I came across approximately sixty years ago in the color rotogravure section of the "New York World Telegraph."

It was in an article about the man who discovered America in 1492, being one of "The Chosen People." The article brought to light newly discovered evidence of the oft pooh-poohed rumor about Christopher Columbus being a Jew. Many thought it to be an old wives' tale, propagated by wishfully thinking old Jews, of which I am one.

The piece went on to suggest that the renowned Italian explorer was born of Jewish parents but had converted to Catholicism in order to secure the funds needed to captain a small fleet of ships. It is not known what his Hebrew name was before he chose to call himself Christopher, the most non-Jewish name extant, or what thinking went into his choice of Columbus for his family name. Whatever it was, this reluctant member of 'the chosen people' chose well enough for Spain's Queen Isabella to fund the equipping of the three vessels that would be under his command.

And in 1492, it came to pass that three ships, The Nina, The Pinta and the Santa Maria, set sail in search of a "new world."

After a long, arduous voyage across the great Atlantic Ocean, Columbus dropped anchor in that "New World off the coast of Jamaica," or as some historians have suggested, "Labrador."

The evidence in the New York World Telegraph's article suggesting that Columbus might have been Jewish, was found in three handwritten letters that passed between Columbus and one of his sons. Imbedded in the third letter, being the most recent to come to light, was the clue that led the journalist to come to the conclusion that he did. In that letter, Columbus' proud son had written,

"Father, you are the first of our people to hold such a vaunted position."

In answer to this, Columbus wrote back,

"Son, you are forgetting David!"

The journalist divined that Columbus was referring to the Old Testament's King David, the second royal leader of The United Kingdom of Israel.

At the bottom of each of their missives, both Columbus and his son had drawn a triangle that contained three Spanish letters, X, M and Y, which resemble three Hebrew letters: Shin, Mem and Ayin. That same words in both languages are found in a triangle at the end of many chapters in the Old Testament-- and those words translated are "Go with God."

Columbus may have very well set sail from Spain in order to survive the Spanish Inquisition. In one of his crew member's letters it was also suggested he had hopes of finding "a homeland for his people," whom he referred to as "Israelites."

Which brings me to a most exciting and illuminating trip abroad that my dear wife Estelle and I went on one summer, many years ago.

On our guided tour of Barcelona, we had the opportunity to see and marvel at Antoni Gaudi's magnificent architecture. The sculpted apartment houses that we viewed on out tour was something we had never before seen.

Continuing on our tour we then came upon an unbelievably impressive, stadium sized, grass-lawned area that Gaudi had designed. The park was rimmed with hundreds of inviting benches that were inlaid with vibrantly colored shards of decorative tiles.

Park Güell Barcelona

What we could never have imagined was another mind blowing structure that Gaudi had built and that our guide insisted we see. He led Estelle and me to one end of the field, where there was an entrance to a stairwell. We followed the guide down a long flight of stairs and when we arrived at the bottom, we saw something that I do not feel equipped to properly describe.

The subterranean area was the same size as the tremendous grassy field above it and it housed a series of beautifully wrought, broad based stone columns that supported the massive park above it.

Since writing about it, I learned that Antoni Gaudi started building the park started in 1900 and finished it in 1914 and officially opened in 1926.

It is a manmade structure that one has to see to believe.

Antoni Gaudi

Our tour of Barcelona was capped with a visit to the Sagrada Familia Cathedral, a hand sculpted structure which Antoni Gaudi started to construct a hundred and thirty-three years ago and which is expected to be finished by 2026.

An amazing aspect of this Cathedral is that it stands in the midst of a community of small houses and narrow streets.

We were about to leave Spain and enter Italy through the port at Padua, which excited us. We had read a great deal about the city and two of its most famous inhabitants, Nicolaus Copernicus and Galileo Galilei.

Our best laid plans almost went awry when we arrived in Padua and discovered that, because it was Sunday, the building which housed both Copernicus and Galileo's laboratories was closed. I literally begged the guard to make an exception and allow us to pay our respect to the two men we so admired. I told him that my wife was an artist and that I was the writer and producer of an important American television series called "The Dick Van Dyke Show," which I knew was stupid of me. I actually considered offering the guard a bribe, but for some reason his face softened and after looking about to see if he would be caught breaking the rules, he bade us "enter."

The tiny, two leveled laboratory we stepped into was nothing we could ever have imagined. It contained two rough hewn desks that were the original ones used by Copernicus and Galileo. Their desks were fashioned from the type of wood often used to crate fruits and vegetables.

Desk of Galileo Galilei

Copernicus, the laboratory's first occupant, died twenty years before Galileo was born.

Copernicus' desk sat at the lower level and Galileo had to climb four steps to get to his. It is hard to imagine that this small workplace once housed two of the greatest minds our world has ever known.

I had read an account of the Spanish Inquisition that occurred in 1492. In that year, Pope Innocent, who presided as head of the Catholic Church, ordered that all Jews be expelled from Spain.

The Romans welcomed these refugees with open arms for, at that time, highwaymen were intercepting and stealing all shipments of gold that were being transported by land. To thwart the thieves the bankers and businessmen stopped shipping their gold by land and started to use letters of credit to transfer their gold by sea. Now, the bankers' major problem was finding workers who were capable of writing and reading these 'letters of credit.'

At that time, most people not literate and most Hebrew males were. Jewish parents felt it was imperative that their sons be taught to read so they would be able to follow the tenets of their Holy Bible.

I also learned that at that time Jews did not have surnames. When asked their names by the border guards, they would answer by saying, "Avram ben Solomon," or "Isaac ben Moshe,"or "Kohlman Ben Shmul"- the word 'ben,' when translated, means 'son of.' It was not until they settled in a town or city that they acquired last names. To their given name was added the name of the town or city to which they had migrated. That is why today many Italian-Americans bear names such as Romano, Italiano, De Ritta, Firenze, Valenti, Napolitano, Sarno, Sebastiani, Sorrentino, Ventura and the like. I know of people who bear these surnames and are not Jewish and unaware that it is likely that their ancestors were.

Back in those ancient days, persons of the Hebrew faith believed they would lead a less arduous life if they converted to Catholicism–and they were right. When it was suggested to the parent of a friend of mine that, because his family bore the surname of an Italian city, Napoli, it is possible that his forbears were Jewish, the parent shook his head and muttered, "Nonsense, nonsense."

In lieu of today's scholarly research, a more fitting response would be, "Sense, sense!"

I would like now to offer kudos to "Linkoln," whose name I bracketed with the other "Kloseted Kike, Kolombus."

I am aware of the title's questionable taste, but there is a part of me that enjoys pushing the 'taste' envelope. I have a rule of thumb about the efficacy of telling something untoward or an off-color joke:

"It is okay, if what one says is funnier than it is dirty-- and makes people laugh."

Once again, it was a newspaper article, this one in the "New York Times," that brought to my attention and, I'm sure, the attention of Jewish folk everywhere-- the possibility that Abraham Lincoln, our 16th President, and his forebears may well have been members of the tribe.

The article described a town in eastern England called Lincoln from which, the writer gleaned, all of Abraham Lincoln's descendants hailed. It was suggested that during the Crusades, the Bishop and Sheriff of Lincoln provided protection for Jewish people. Even though the Jews were officially expelled from England in 1290, some converted to Christianity and were designated as 'Conversos.' It is not known if Lincoln's ancestors were among those who remained in England and feigned being converted but preserved their Hebraic traditions.

President Lincoln never professed to be of the Jewish faith or any faith but, when asked about his beliefs, he would refer to the Ten Commandments in the Hebrew Bible.

During his term in office many of his closest friends and advisors were Jewish, among them a lawyer, Abraham Jonas, a prominent doctor, Isacshar Zacharie, and a New York Rabbi, M.J. Raphall of the Congregation B'nai Jushurun.

Another Rabbi, Isaac Mayer Wise, wrote that, "In my presence Lincoln confided his Jewish heritage."

It was noted that Lincoln was the first United States President to permit rabbis to serve as Jewish Chaplains in the United States Armed Forces.

During the Civil War, when General Ulysses S. Grant expelled Tennessee Jews from a district controlled by the North, President Lincoln revoked the anti-Semitic edict.

General Ulysses S. Grant

In reality, all the above does not prove anything about Lincoln's religion. Had he been Jewish, it is more likely that Honest Abe would not have hidden his heritage.

Someone once argued, "Look, his given name is Abraham and he looks Jewish, that's good enough for me!"

Abraham Lincoln, our 16th President

DisWilliam

Buffy

The Mating of Mary Tyler Moore's and My Dog

or

Mis-Matched Mutts

Carl & Mary, 1964

CHAPTER TWENTY-FOUR

The Mating of Mary Tyler Moore's and My Dog or Mis-Matched Mutts

It was in 1967 or 1968 that Mary Tyler Moore and her then husband, Grant Tinker, resided in Beverly Hills-- the Tinkers on Beverly Drive and the Reiners, just around the corner, on Rodeo Drive. Both the Tinkers and the Reiners owned pet dogs. Ours was a beagle named Buffy, theirs a Bichon Frise named 'Diswilliam' which, in English, translates to 'This William.' To this day, when I go for my daily stroll and pass the former Tinker abode, I mutter, "Diswilliam did abide 'dere'!"

I 'm not sure, but I believe it was at a chance meeting at the market, when Mary mentioned that she wished her dog had a female partner 'to love' instead of their newly upholstered ottoman. It was fated that we meet, as our Buffy was in heat and Estelle and I had talked about finding a mate for her. To jump start their coupling, we suggested that Mary bring Diswilliam to our home that day.

For their romantic encounter, we chose a small cement area right outside our kitchen door. The two animals, though of different breeds, were alike in size--Diswilliam, a mite smaller and much furrier.

It was obvious by their behavior that they were both eager to "get it on!" I use that term advisedly because as soon as they met, they tried to 'get it on,' but neither seemed to know anything about the procedure. They circled each other, sniffed each other and unsuccessfully tried to mount each other. Mary and I cheered them on but cheering was not going to get it done. At one point, Diswilliam actually did mount Buffy and started to hump her head. It was here I felt I must intervene and, gingerly, I picked up the eager stud and placed him at the proper end.

After a few aborted attempts, Mary and I decided that they needed our help, and we actually picked up our pets and placed the panting participants in the proper position to do the deed. It took no longer than a minute before Diswilliam dismounted and ran to the other end of the enclosure.

We had no idea that Buffy was impregnated, but had to wait no longer than three months for her to deliver six of the smallest, cutest mixed breed puppies in the world.

Four of the six were more than two handfuls

And what a good and caring mother Buffy was! For the following eight weeks, she did nothing but lie around and nurse her half dozen offspring, who, each hour, seemed to grow bigger. At the end of eight weeks, we saw Buffy behave in a way we had never before seen.

We were on the back lawn and she was being followed by her hungry brood. The little mongrels were waiting for her to lie down so that they could nurse, but instead of lying down, Buffy ran from them until she was about thirty or forty feet away-- she then put her head down as if she were a ram, charged and butted one of her pups hard enough to knock him over.

Buffy repeated these head butts until each of the pups understood that they were being weaned. My wife understood, and immediately started filling their watering bowls with milk and dog food.

As the mixed breed pups grew, it was quite apparent that they were a breed apart. We offered the "pick of the litter" to everyone we knew-- relatives, friends, acquaintances, but no one found any of our little mongrels worth picking.

I began to worry and, to abort the possibility of permanently being a 'seven dog household,' I placed ads in both "Daily Variety" and "The Hollywood Reporter," informing their readers that six darling, celebrity-owned, Beagle-Bichon Frise puppies were available for immediate adoption, and I signed my 'celebrity' name, Carl Reiner. I was happily surprised that 'celebrity owned' pups were just what folks wanted to adopt. In one day, we found a new home for each of Buffy's litter.

Estelle and I were always happy to receive postcards from our pups' owners telling us how well Buffy's kids were doing.

For the record, Buffy lived to the ripe old age of thirteen which, in dog years, is ninety-one.

Buffy at 42

Our old backyard Ficus Benjimina in her hey day.

Old Ficus & Young Magnolia-
A Sad Happy Tale of Two Trees

48 Bonnie Meadow Rd. New Rochelle, NY

CHAPTER TWENTY-FIVE

Old Ficus & Young Magnolia- A Sad Happy Tale of Two Trees

The year was 1961, the skies were blue and circumstances, brought about by my choosing a career in show business, made it necessary for my wife and me to move from New Rochelle to Los Angeles. At that time we were in the process of finding a home for our family, which boasted a handsome twelve year old son, Rob, a pretty ten year old daughter, Annie, and Lucas, the cutest eleven month old extant. We had just moved from the east coast where I had no steady job, to the west coast where I had two steady jobs, one performing on "The Dinah Shore Show," and the other, producing "The Dick Van Dyke Show."

Until then for almost a year we had been living in a rented house in Beverly Hills on North Alta Drive, and it was important that we find a house that would not require our children to make yet another change of schools–to that end, we searched for a home in Beverly Hills.

Estelle, a fine artist and a licensed architectural draftsman, had a definite sense of the kind of house in which our family would be aesthetically and physically comfortable. To say that we visited twenty or more houses would be only a slight exaggeration. It seems that the architects who designed homes after the nineteen fifties had decided that the concept of rooms with doors was archaic. Rooms were replaced by areas, living areas, door-less dining room areas, door-less kitchen, living room and bedroom areas–none of which we found hospitable or habitable. Estelle and I preferred the old fashioned abodes that offered warm, cozy rooms with warm, lockable and un-lockable doorknobbed doors.

We were just about ready to give up on finding something that suited our needs, when the realtor opened the front door of a house on Rodeo Drive. We took one step into the foyer, and as long as it takes to say, "We'll take it!"–we said "We'll take it!" and we took it.

Dead ahead, we saw a fifteen foot hallway, an ample sized living room, through whose glass doors at the end of the room, we had a view of a good sized backyard, a swimming pool and a small, shingle roofed pool house.

To the left we saw a dining room that had a sliding door, and next to the dining room was a door to the kitchen. To our right was a living room that had two double hinged folding doors.

Even before the real estate agent, Florie Shayne, escorted us upstairs to see the four bedrooms and den, we had made up our minds. This was to be our new home!

One other lovely feature that the second floor offered was an outdoor L shaped patio that could be accessed by going out a screened door in the fourth bedroom. From that patio, we had two separate views,-the long part of the L afforded us a panoramic view of our backyard and pool, and the shorter part offered us easy access to a tree that bore delicious, seedless, navel oranges.

Our backyard's main attraction was a very large tree, a Ficus Benjamina–which I had learned was a pedestrian variety of Ficus. The limbs and leaves of our healthy Ficus made for a giant umbrella-like sun shade, making it the center for more than one joyous occasion–they being the marriages of our eldest child, Rob, to Penny Marshall and our youngest, Lucas, to Maude Winchester.

Maude & Lucas

For each of these weddings, approximately one hundred of our relatives and friends gathered, which included my father, my brother Charlie and his wife Ilse. I still smile when I recall Rob and Penny's outdoor wedding lunch that Rob and Penny had chosen to be catered by Ah Fong's, a down scale Chinese restaurant. The hot meal was served to guests who sat at cloth covered card tables. A variety of this downscale restaurant's signature dishes were delivered in large, cardboard take-out type containers. It was a delicious meal and reflected the bride and groom's background, culinary elan and sense of humor. I will never forget the 3 by 5 inch slip of lined paper the delivery boy handed me. It was the food bill and scribbled on it were three words,'Food to go,' and the price, $695.

The beloved Ficus tree was also central to many, many backyard lunches and swim parties.

People pass on, as do their pets. Sadly, our home was central to too many of those sad occasions. What we had never experienced was the death of a massive, seemingly invulnerable tree. This past summer, our sturdy, fully-leafed, wedding canopy started to die. It took but a few months for an incurable rot to set in and cause a giant limb to tumble into the courtyard. I asked our gardener, Juan Aquino, if he would cut it down and replace it. Mr. Aquino said that he would try to find another one for me and I told him that I did not want to replace it with another Ficus, but a Magnolia. My dear departed wife had once chosen to plant a 6-foot Magnolia tree to grace the front yard of our new home in New Rochelle.

Annie, Robbie & New Magnolia

For seven years, until we moved to California, we saw our little Magnolia tree grow and bloom. Years later, when Robbie and Annie were adults, they paid a visit to our old home and reported that our little Magnolia tree was now a giant Magnolia tree, taller than the house, and its blooms were bigger and more beautiful than ever.

When I asked Juan Aquino if he knew where to get a large Magnolia tree, I expected him to say "Sorry," but he surprised me by saying that he had recently removed one from a customer's yard and had stored it in his nursery.

A day later, a huge truck, carting the giant tree, drove up my driveway and into my backyard. Following was a station wagon with a crew of men, who immediately started sawing down the dead Ficus. Their most arduous task was digging out the tree's massive stump and its network of deeply embedded roots.

It took the better part of two days before the dogged workers dug a hole deep enough to accommodate the giant, canvas-balled roots of the twenty foot high Magnolia tree.

Thanks to Juan Aquino and his men, this full-leafed beauty has now lived in our backyard for a few months. So far, there are no signs of buds.

Cherry Blossoms

I hope when next spring rolls around, our Magnolia tree will emulate its Washington D.C. cousins, The Cherry Blossoms, and gift us with large, magnificent Magnolias.

How Ronald Colman and Greer Garson Make Mush Out of Me

Ronald Colman in
"A Tale Of Two Cities," 1935

CHAPTER TWENTY-SIX

How Ronald Colman and Greer Garson Make Mush Out of Me

All who know me are aware that I have admired Ronald Colman for most of my life. In my first semi-autobiographic novel, "Enter Laughing," the young aspiring actor, David Kokolowitz, so admires Ronald Colman that he actually changes his name to Don Colman.

As a young teenager, when I first became aware of this handsome, silken voiced, British actor who starred in "A Tale of Two Cities," "The Prisoner Of Zenda," "Lost Horizons" and "Random Harvest," I wanted to be him. To this day, if asked, I can still do a creditable impression of Mr. Colman reciting the final lines of Dickens' "A Tale of Two Cities:"

"It is a far, far better thing that I do than I have ever done; it is a far, far better rest I go to, than I have ever known."

A year or so ago, on one of the cable channels, I had the opportunity to revisit "Random Harvest," a film I had loved since it's release in 1942. I had such a strong visceral reaction to viewing the film that I was prompted to buy a copy of it. I immediately invited a young couple who had never seen the film to watch it with me. I promised them that they were about to see one of the most romantic films ever made and that they "would be moved to tears."

We watched the film and, during the final credits, I found that I had not over sold "Random Harvest-" they were not only moved to tears but shed a few.

I have since then shown the film to my sophisticated and brilliant daughter, Dr. Annie Reiner, and gotten the same reaction. Mel Brooks, who knows a few things about writing, producing and directing films knew exactly when and how much to tear up.

Why, you may ask, am I singing such loud praises for a film in which, I swear, I have no vested interest?

My 'praise singing' is a trait that dates back to my early days as a Master of Ceremonies, when I derived great pleasure by addressing audiences and introducing performers whose skills begot approbation, applause and once in awhile, a standing ovation. Not only did I enjoy the performers' skills, but vicariously, I enjoyed the fact that it was I who had brought the audience's attention to that performer.

In my bedroom, at this very moment, a copy of "Random Harvest" sits in my DVD player. Oft times after watching news reports about worldwide atrocities interspersed with ads that explain how beneficial and dangerous it is to take Viagra, I switch off the news, click on "Random Harvest," and watch a particular scene that is 'cued up.'

It is a scene early in the film where Greer Garson is performing on a stage wearing a fetching plaid kilt skirt that features her shapely legs. Prancing gracefully about the stage, she raucously sings a Scottish ditty about a gal named "Daisy" who was quite a "Doooooozy!"

It is in my role as your Master Of Ceremonies that I urge all you 'gentle readers' and 'tough readers' to buy, borrow or rent a DVD of "Random Harvest." Then, with a loved one at your side, or even a liked one, hit the play button and allow the film to work it's romantic magic.

So, there you have it! If I have motivated anyone to watch a DVD of one of my all time favorite films, then I will have successfully fulfilled my role as a Master of Ceremonies.

How to Extend Your Life Expectancy

CHAPTER TWENTY-SEVEN

How to Extend Your Life Expectancy

Today the most renowned scientists and technicians are working long hours to discover a method to increase the length and quality of human life. These dedicated men and women have successfully created and manufactured drugs that have added years to the lives of people whose genetic make-up tended to point to a relatively shorter life span.

A few months ago, I found in my mailbox more than the usual amount of flyers from local food markets and catalogues from our nation's overstocked mail order houses. My late beloved wife, Estelle, besides be-loving me, loved to leaf through these catalogues. They came in handy during the holidays and she used them to do most of her gift shopping. She would circle items, such as scarves, bathrobes, hats, toys, sweaters, slippers, dresses and crockery and have them delivered to our home. She would then properly wrap and tag them, put them under our tree or have them delivered to those who lived out of town.

Of the dozens of catalogues I received this year, there was none from Norm Thompson, whose catalogue I desperately needed. I had once bought a pair of pants from them that fit me like the proverbial glove. I think these trousers were called "Sans-A-Belt" but I am not sure–what I do know is that if these were the only trousers I ever owned that did not require a belt to keep them aloft. I have many in my closet but nowhere on them is a label with its name. When I say I have many "Sans-A-Belts", I mean upwards of twenty. Wait! I think maybe they're called "Auto-Sizers." Whatever they're called, I'm ordering six of them!

'Having new trousers hanging in my closet, ready to be worn,' I thought, 'would be an incentive to stay healthy and active.' I pictured myself strutting down the aisles of Whole Foods and showing off my newly bought pants. It would be unconscionable and foolhardy of me not live long enough to get my money's worth. For that reason, it is important that I hang around a tad longer -or preferably, a ton of tads longer.'

In Chapter eight, when writing about Tyrone Power, I described a fifth synchronistic moment that befell me and I swore on the largest stack of Bible-like books that what I had written was the unvarnished, truthiest of truths.

Well, today, in this chapter, I am going to offer another synchronistic event that came my way. On that same stack of Bible-like books, I swear to you that the moment that I was thinking about how I might buy some new beltless trousers, Sally Mamom, my housekeeper, quietly came into my office and placed the day's mail on my desk. I, as many writers admit, live for interruptions and look for reasons to goof off.

Today, the interruptive activity with which I busied myself was scanning the junk mail that was just delivered. I trashed all the ads and all the letters that solicit donations to charities in which I have no interest, or ones I do support and have recently sent contributions. After tossing out six or seven catalogues featuring women's apparel, I was on the verge of discarding one from, you guessed it, Norm Thompson. I flipped it open and, I swear, on its third page were photos that featured my sought after elastic pants, the one designated not as "Auto-Sizer" or "Sans-A-Belt," but as "Always Fit."

Ha Ha! "Always Fit!!" I shouted and then ordered six pair!

These six beltless beauties now proudly hang in my bedroom closet where they share a rack with their older peers–all eagerly awaiting the opportunity to assist me in extending my life expectancy.*

* I just realized that as I write this, I am actually wearing the "Always-fit" trousers pictured on the previous page.

Norm Thompson
escape from the ordinary
Tijuana
TEXAS
(U.S.A.)
M
E
X
I
C
O
N
San Miguel
Guadalajara
Mexico City
Acapulco
Cancun
Art Direction Award winn
2006 Applied Arts Magazine
MEN'S
COLLECTION
normthompson.com | Segue to San Miguel | June 2006

My Photo in The Obit Section All But Ruined My Breakfast

Los Angeles Times
A29
OBITUARIES
Emmy-winning actress, club singer
OBITUARY NOTICES

CHAPTER TWENTY-EIGHT

My Photo in The Obit Section All But Ruined My Breakfast

I am sure that somewhere in the not too distant past I have written about what I say to myself every morning after I sit down at the breakfast table and open my newspaper. For the millions who are not privy to those words, they are:

"If my name is not listed in the Obituary section, I'll have breakfast."

Well, this morning, as is my wont, I followed my schedule and, lo and behold, prominently displayed in the Obit section was a smiling photo of me standing next to Polly Bergen. I read the first two words of the headline, "Emmy Winning-" and froze for a millisecond before realizing that it was Polly Bergen, a lovely and talented compatriot, who had passed away. I cannot, for the life of me, imagine why the Obit editor could not find a solo shot of Polly Bergen, an excellent actress who had starred in dozens of hit motion pictures, among them, "Cape Fear" and "The Winds Of War"-- plus having had a long and successful career as a television hostess and panelist.

For one fleeting moment I wondered, 'When I go, with what living celebrity might that Obit editor pair me?'

Ah, to be honest, I did not think that at all, but when one is blessed or cursed with a mind bent toward humor, it is hard to control oneself.

To look on the bright side of a dark subject, I now feel that when my time does arrive to be featured in an obituary, the Obit editor will choose a suitable photo to accompany what, I imagine, will be a laudatory article that covers the high points of my life and career. I am not in a position to approve or disapprove, but if that creative editor decides to include others in my 'phinal' photo, I suggest he use Estelle or our wedding photo, or photos of me with my children and grandchildren. Or even this smiling shot of a young Mel Brooks that appeared on Page 26 in my 2013 bio, "I Remember Me."

Honeymoon Heaven,
a Three Room Suite in Neosho, Mo.

CHAPTER TWENTY-NINE

Honeymoon Heaven, a Three Room Suite in Neosho, Mo.

Hanging on the wall of the twelve yard corridor that leads from my bedroom to my office are paintings, large and small, that I have passed by for fifty years or more. Among the hangings are oil portraits, a few still lifes, two or three abstracts and one portrait of me in uniform that my wife, a graduate of the National Academy of Arts, did when I was stationed in Camp Crowder, Missouri. It is a flattering likeness of the 22 year old me that she dared to attempt to do in water color–and she succeeded. Unlike oils, a water color painting cannot be altered if there are things that need altering--like the size of the subject's nose, ears and lips or the color of their skin or hair. To do any of the above, Estelle would have had to trash what she had done, and start anew using a fresh sheet of paper–but she needed but one sheet to capture me.

Yesterday morning, for no reason at all, I thought of that water color Estelle had painted of me during our two week idyllic post honeymoon in Neosho, Mo. We had our original honeymoon in Washington, D.C. while I attended Georgetown University.

The water color conjured up the memory of the backyard of a small house in Neosho, Missouri, and the room in it that we had rented. Our quarters were part of a three room apartment which we shared with two other newlywed couples. Estelle and I occupied the first room one came upon when entering the apartment. Couple number two had to go through our room to get to theirs and the third couple had to go through our room and couple two's room to get to their room. Why and how the apartments were laid out like a train, only the failed architect would know.

The room Estelle and I called home had its advantages and its disadvantages. Its advantage was that it was the closest to the one toilet that all six of us would share. And its disadvantages were that four people would be walking past our bed every night and all seemed to have weak bladders.

From dusk to dawn there was a steady stream of newlyweds who had to pass by our bed to get to where they needed to go. Unless we were exhibitionists, romantic coupling for us front room honeymooners was out of the question.

I must admit that our apartment mates were actually very thoughtful, for when the need arose for them to visit the tiny toilet, nary a footstep was heard. These silent treks went on for a night or two before Estelle and I realized that the precious time we had left to spend together, and the activities in which we wished to partake, needed to be addressed forthwith!

Estelle, being a graduate of the National Academy of Art and having been employed by Sperry Rand Corporation as an architectural draftsman, had me rig a curtain that she designed. Using nothing more than some twine, a hammer, a couple of nails and a bed sheet, we were able to screen from view anything that might be going on behind it.

After writing that last sentence, I thought about those two couples and wondered if they are still alive, and if they are, might they chance to read this and get a chuckle out of it.

I also thought about our visiting the Bronx neighborhood from which we sprung... and her looking up at the building she lived in as a teenager.

Another thought hit me-- the water color that Estelle painted of me in uniform would make a great cover for this book–it does, doesn't it?

And after writing that last, last sentence I thought about something that made me chuckle. Many times in my life I have said the following words about my wife; "Estelle raised three great kids and one great husband," and this morning when going to the market, I listened to a recording Estelle made of the Helen Humes classic, "Million Dollar Secret."

Here now is the final stanza of that song–its penultimate line accurately captured the nature of our sixty-five year relationship;
"Now take a look in the barnyard
See that old fat hen
She's got a fresh young rooster
Feels just like a chick again
So get a young man, and raise him to your hand
He'll make you think life is wonderful, yes you'll think the world is grand."

That is precisely what twenty-eight year old Estelle Lebost did in Nineteen forty-two after wedding twenty-one year old Carl Reiner–she raised him to her hand and made him not think that life was wonderful, but know that life is wondeful and that 'the world is grand.'

If I'm to Be an Actress,
I Should Learn How to Act

CHAPTER THIRTY

If I'm to Be an Actress, I Should Learn How to Act

The thirteen words in the above title were uttered in 1980 by my wife Estelle, and the one responsible for her considering that path was her friend, Academy Award winning actress, Anne Bancroft.

Two years earlier, Anne who, as a performer, had conquered both Broadway and Hollywood, became interested in broadening her horizons. To that end she wrote a couple of one act plays. One of those plays, "The August," was the vehicle that not only gave birth to Anne's career as a writer-director, but Estelle's career as an actress.

In the play, which would be performed for a few nights at the AFI theater, Anne asked her friend to play a small part, that of an adoring theater fan who asks a Broadway star for her autograph. The part which required her to step on a stage and deliver but two short lines was, for Estelle, a life changing experience.

At that time, with our children grown, Estelle's primary interest was getting to do what she should have been doing all her life, singing! She loved to sing the blues and after much preparation she finally got to it. Once a month, for the next sixteen years, she sang all manner of Jazz and Blues songs at the Gardenia Supper Club in Los Angeles. She made occasional forays to New York, where she performed at the Café Carlyle and one time at the famous "Michael's Pub."

At that time, Estelle was also afforded the opportunity to perform on Johnny Carson's "The Tonight Show," "The Merv Griffin Show," and "The Regis Philbin Show."

Soon after writing and directing "The August," Anne Bankcroft's small film, Anne lent her talents to writing, directing and performing in "Fatso," a full length film in which she cast Dom Deluise to play the title role, Candy Azzara to play his girlfriend, Ron Carey played his brother, and Estelle Reiner, a neighborhood acquaintance. Estelle had a couple of short scenes, one as a customer purchasing a birthday card in Dom's gift shop and another where she advised Dom that for his health and longevity he consider joining her weight loss class, the "Chubby Checkers."

Dom Deluise & Estelle Reiner in "Fatso"

After an early screening of the film, Anne Bancroft, who had been a member of The Actors Studio, asked her mentor, Lee Strasberg, if he had any thoughts about the film or the actors. She told Estelle that Strasberg said that the only member of her cast that seemed real to him was the woman who came into your shop and bought a greeting card.

Armed with that rave review, and the excitement of doing something she knew little about, Estelle said, "If I am going to be an actress, I better learn how."

Soon after, she applied to "The Actors Studio" and audited Lee Strasberg's classes.

Not long after, Mel Brooks, impressed by Estelle's performance in "Fatso," offered her the opportunity to play the part of a wardrobe mistress in his new film, "To Be Or Not To Be." The fact that Mel hired her to do that part has miraculously added much joy to my present life.

One night, about two weeks ago, after brushing my teeth and settling into my bed I clicked on my TV and instead of watching the late night talk shows, I scrolled down the list of shows I had recorded, and chose to watch the Mel Brooks version of the classic, anti-Nazi film, "To Be Or Not to Be." It turned out to be a very special night for me. What made it special was a particular scene where a character, played by Tim Matheson, comes to a theater's stage door to warn the crew and the performers that Nazi storm troopers are coming to arrest all the show's Jewish personnel. Estelle, the wardrobe mistress, opens the door, sees it is the leading lady's lover and starts to smile. By pressing the pause button on my remote control, I captured that smile and thus made it possible for me, before nodding off, to say a fond good night to my sweet, smiling wife.

How 1000 lbs of Walnuts with Nuts Inside Their Shells Can Be Worth Less to Me Than One Walnut with No Nut Inside

THANK YOU,
CARL, FOR A
WONDERFUL
STORY.
ELAINE
AND SAUL

CHAPTER THIRTY-ONE

How 1000 lbs of Walnuts with Nuts Inside Their Shells Can Be Worth Less To Me Than One Walnut with No Nut Inside

Had not the name Saul Bass come up in a conversation with my publisher, I would not have opened a rarely opened desk drawer and found the walnut that begot the longest chapter title in this book.

Saul Bass, as film buffs are aware, was one of the truly great designers of movie main titles and special sequences. In his forty year career he lent his artistic hand to such iconic films as: "North By Northwest," "Cape Fear," "Vertigo," "Anatomy Of A Murder," "Psycho," "Spartacus" and "It's A Mad, Mad, Mad, Mad World," a film to which we both contributed, he, a lot and I, very little.

I had met Saul when we were lending our left wing efforts to do worthwhile political activities like opposing the war in Vietnam, but we had not, as they say, hung out together. It was some time after that he sent me a gift wrapped box that contained one walnut.

For those who missed seeing the fine episode of "The Dick Van Dyke Show" I wrote in 1963, that was titled, "It May Look Like A Walnut," here is why Saul Bass gifted me with a single walnut.

I was quite proud of the walnut show because I had been searching fruitlessly for an idea that would be different than anything we had done in the last three seasons, when suddenly an image of Rod Serling and the "Twilight Zone" popped into my head. I became excited at the prospect of doing a satire of that popular futuristic show. Ordinarily, it would take three to five days for me to write a half hour episode, but "It May Look Like A Walnut" flew out of my typewriter in one Sunday afternoon.

Every Wednesday morning at Desilu Studios, before starting rehearsals for our current show, our cast and crew would gather around an oblong table and do a cold reading of the following week's script. I was particularly excited about this show, and was hoping that the cast and our executive producer, Sheldon Leonard, would share my enthusiasm. I don't rightly remember what reactions Dick, Mary, Rosemarie or Morey had, but I will never forget Sheldon's. He picked up the script, shook his head and unceremoniously tossed it on the table. He said something to the effect that it needed to go back to the drawing board–which was exactly the opposite of how I felt. I knew that I had a winner and I defended my script by saying that it had elements that were new for us. Besides the episode spoofing "The Twilight Zone," the "Walnut" in our show was also a satire of the pod used in "The Body Snatchers," a film about spooky aliens that invade our planet, snatch humans and absorb their bodies into giant plant-like pods.

Ninety percent of the time Sheldon Leonard and I agreed about the subject and content of our scripts but this time Sheldon and I adamantly disagreed.

"Sheldon," I insisted, "this is one of the best scripts I've ever written." and he countered by saying, "Well this 'best script' of yours is not worth shooting, dump it!"

I naturally defended my work, and after a couple more contrapuntal exchanges, Sheldon shrugged, said, "It's your baby," flipped his yellow Ticonderoga pencil onto the table and walked off.

There were many elements of the show that were entertaining and unexpected, one being how when Robert Petrie, Dick Van Dyke's character, morphs into a Twilo-ite, he loses two things that Twilo-ite's don't have, thumbs and a sense of humor! Another entertaining element was the visiting extraterrestrial from the planet "Twilo." This alien is described as looking exactly like Danny Thomas, and the role was played by comedian Danny Thomas.

Danny Thomas as an alien from Twilo on The Dick Van Dyke Show

A major problem that still confronted us was the securing of the walnuts. When our prop master, Glen Ross, learned that we would be needing 'a whole lot of walnuts' for the show, he naively asked, "A whole lot? What kind of 'whole lot "are you talking about, five pounds, ten pounds–how many?"

"Enough to fill up the clothes closet in our foyer," I answered.

Glen did not bat an eyelash. He picked up the phone, found the number for "The Diamond Walnut Company," discussed with them the size or our closet and learned that they would be happy to fill our closet with 1000 lbs. of nonreturnable walnuts. They then asked what we wanted to do with the unreturnable nuts. We chose to invite the cast and crew to take home as many nuts as they wanted, and the rest we would donate to some charitable organization that may be low on walnuts. As an incentive, they were told that the walnuts were used in The Dick Van Dyke Show.

A word about Sheldon Leonard, when a news reporter interviewed about his role as an executive producer of "T and L Productions" he brought up our show's "Walnut" episode and admitted that he had been dead wrong in his assessment of that episode and his recommendation to scrap it. Proving once again that he was a true 'mensh.' (Yiddish for 'a good and caring person')

Among the many viewers who saw the original episode when it was telecast was the estimable Saul Bass, who was moved to send me a package that contained a single walnut, and between its shells was not a crunchy nut, but a tiny piece of paper shaped like a thumb less hand. On the palm of the teeny hand was the teeniest handwritten note, that I needed a magnifying glass to read:

"Thank you Carl for a wonderful story, Elaine and Saul Bass."

The fact that fifty two years ago I received that walnuted note and can access it in a second, attests to the my appreciation of Saul's 'thank you' gift.

FYI: Those who wish to see a 1000 pound tidal wave of walnuts cascade out of a clothes closet with Mary Tyler Moore's body surfing on it, Google, "It May Look Like A Walnut" and view that scene and the entire show!

WNYC

When Mayor Fiorello H. LaGuardia Praised My Fine Work

Bound in 1935, copies of my father's Popular Science magazines

CHAPTER THIRTY-TWO

When Mayor Fiorello H. LaGuardia Praised My Fine Work

I was certain that, after fortuitously finding the Saul Bass designed walnut in my desk drawer, and relating a story about a closet filled with 1000 pounds of walnuts, I had written what I had intended to be the final chapter of this book—but I was wrong! The following day, I am not sure how his name came up, but there I was thinking about Fiorello LaGuardia and how I chanced to meet him seventy-nine years ago.

I was thirteen at the time and attending Bronx's Angelo Patri Junior High School # 45. I spent two years in junior high school where students who were considered to be above average were able to trim a full year off their elementary school education before going on to High School.

At my junior high, we were required to attend a "shop class" where we would learn to do manual work such as furniture building, book binding and vegetable gardening. I was lucky to be assigned to the book binding class, where I not only learned how to bind a book but I had the opportunity to chat with one of our country's most outstanding citzens.

It was while busily binding a book that I heard this man's voice ask:

"Young man, what are you doing?"

"Book binding," I answered.

"Well, you seem to be doing fine work. Keep at it."

That man, with whom I chatted, was standing directly behind me-- it was our Mayor, Fiorello LaGuardia, and the "fine work" I was in the process of doing was joining six of seven of my father's favorite magazines, "Popular Science" and "Science & Mechanics," into a hard covered book.

During World War I, Mayor LaGuardia was a fighter pilot who later was awarded many decorations for his heroism. In 1934 he was elected New York City's Mayor and he served three more terms. He may well have been the most beloved Mayor that New York, or any city, has ever had.

To illustrate that, during a newspaper strike, youngsters were deprived of reading the Sunday 'funnies,' and our hands-on mayor took it upon himself to do something about it. He sat behind a microphone at a local radio station and read the Sunday Funnies to a city full of entranced and happy children. He used different, comical voices for the likes of "Mutt and Jeff," "Popeye," "Olive Oyl," "Mickey Mouse" and "The Katzenjammer Kids."

Mayor Fiorello LaGuardia broadcasting the Sunday comic strips

I, and many thousand of kids, heard our Mayor reading these comics, and I'll wager that those of us who are still 'hanging in' will never forget it.

Now, to what spurred me to get excited about writing this chapter. It was my being reminded of the old science magazines that my father never tossed out and that I chose to bind into books. It has been years since I had handled one of these 'books' and last week I searched them out. I remember putting them on a book shelf in our living room and I was happy see them stacked right next to the outdated set of The Encyclopedia Britannica. All six of the covers of my bound "Popular Mechanics" and "Popular Science" magazines were a light shade of green.

In a couple of these bound books, I had slipped little strips of paper to mark something that I thought interesting. I opened one and saw a photo of the new 1933 Plymouth Six Automobile that was priced at four hundred and forty-five dollars.

In another I found, between the pages, a pink cloth that was once used for wiping smudges off eyeglass lenses. The two by three pink cloth bore the name and address of an optometrist, Dr. H.M. Reiner, my father's brother and my uncle Harry. I opened the book to where, years ago, I had placed this marker and was surprised to find at the bottom of a page, a small photo of a young boy looking through some sort of a stereotypical device. I had, a millennia ago, when I was six or eight years old, looked through that very same device. My father had taken our family to visit my uncle's office in midtown Manhattan to see the new invention he had just patented–one that was capable of straightening the eyes of cross-eyed and wall-eyed children without resorting to expensive and invasive surgery.

In this stereotypical device, my uncle placed two photos, one of a bird and one of a cage and he would ask his young clients to try, by crossing their eyes, to get the bird into the cage. At each session, by repeating this exercise over and over again they were, after a several visits, able to look at their family and friends straight in the eye.

CROSS-EYES NOW CURED BY PICTURES

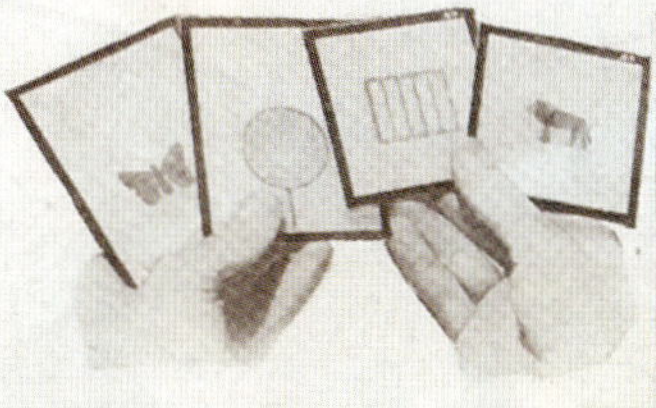

Attractive picture cards, above, are used in the new method of curing cross-eyed children without an operation

With the stereoscope-like instrument, right, the cross-eyed patient tries to make two pictures fuse together

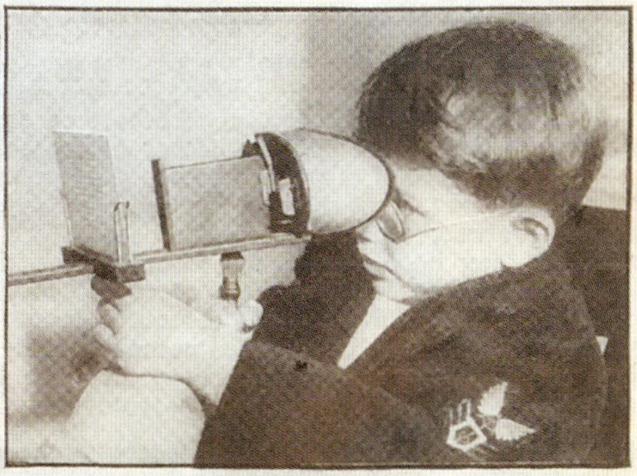

CURING cross-eyes is play for youthful patients at a New York eye clinic, opened recently. A child places a pair of attractive picture slides in an instrument resembling an old-fashioned stereoscope and manipulates the device to make the pictures fuse together. Thus he tries to trap a lion in a cage or catch a butterfly in a net. Through corrective exercises of this sort, a cure is often effected without recourse to a surgical operation, which hitherto was nearly always considered necessary.

In the small item printed in that "Popular Science Magazine," there was a description of the invention but no mention of the inventor's name which, I am happy to advise, was Optometrist Dr. Harry M. Reiner, who, in 1933 had an office that was located at 47 West 34th Street, New York N.Y- Tel. Wisconsin 7-2457.

Inventing things was something my father, my Uncle Harry and my grandfather Simon had in their genes.

My Uncle Harry and his look-a-like brother, my father, Irving

My father, Irving Reiner invented and patented a clock that ran for two years on a five cent-battery-- which was the shelf life of the battery. He also received a patent for a dry pile battery that could deliver four thousand volts and a milli-amp that, without re-charging, kept a pendulum clock running for sixty consecutive years. He also had drawn the plans and specifications for the development of the self-winding wristwatch.

My Uncle Harry, besides the crossed-eye curing device, invented and manufactured a 'clog free' salt shaker and sugar dispenser that was successfully marketed at the seashore and other high moisture areas.

In the later 1800's my grandfather Simon Reiner, a master watchmaker, invented the first wind-up toy car.

I have a hunch that in ancient times, the Reiner clan harbored many more inventors, and I am excited about Dr. Louis Gates' offer to search out the genealogical history of our family. If anything of interest is found, he has invited me to appear on his television show.

And if he does...check your local listings.

Beverly
Cinema
CARL REINER
IN PERSON

The Highest Paying Job Ever Offered to Me or Any Actor in Theatrical History

My loyal and trusted manager George Shapiro... also, Jerry Seinfeld's

CHAPTER THIRTY-THREE

The Highest Paying Job Ever Offered to Me or Any Actor in Theatrical History

This high paying offer to perform a small role came to me but a fortnight ago and it was an offer that I, or any actor, would have to be out of his or her mind to refuse.

On first learning of it, I thought it was some sort of practical joke and possibly an anti-Semitic one but when I realized that the intriguing, albeit nutty offer was emailed to me by my loyal and trusted manager, George Shapiro, I realized that it was a valid offer. The original offer was made by a gentleman I did not know, a Neil Senturia and I thought you might enjoy experiencing what I did when I received it. To that end and for optimum dramatic effect, I will not divulge the financial details of the offer until the end of this, one of the shortest chapter in the book.

If, perchance, you are one who, when reading a 'who done it' cannot resist 'sneaking a peek' at the last page to find out 'who done it,' please do not feel constrained to fight your nature. However, to help those who would prefer to 'fight their nature,' but can't, the words of the offer are already printed at the very bottom of this page in the smallest type available-- so small that to read it without using a strong magnifying glass would be well nigh impossible. Hoping that you will not try to read it, I continue.

A day after receiving this dramatic offer, I found myself watching a group of skilled technicians set up state-of-the-art recording equipment in my living room. In less than ten minutes the director shouted "Role tape!," bade me to perform, which I did. He then shouted, "That's a wrap!," thanked me for my cooperation and left.

Now, if you have not tried or did try and failed, you can, by turning the page, learn the details of Neil Senturia's "highest paying job offer ever."

Mr. Reiner, we are offering you five thousand dollars to record the word, "Oy!"

"Mr. Reiner we are offering you five thousand dollars to record the word "Oy!"

Naturally I accepted the offer but never quite understood how the producers were planning to use my recorded "Oy!" I was told that my "Oy!" would be accessed on an app. I assumed that computer-literate folk who know what an app is, will access the app and when these modern folk are upset at something or somebody, they can use me as a surrogate 'Oyer' to shout or sigh an "Oy!" for them.

Does that make any sense? Probably not but neither does receiving twenty-five hundred dollars a letter to perform a two letter word! Oy!

I will in one month and one week be entering into my ninety-third year on this earth and wonder what new, slightly confusing and not-really-needed new gimmick, gadget or what have you will I have to learn about and almost master.

Note: The week after receiving payment, for saying "Oy!," my gnawing guilt was successfully assuaged by upping my contributions to the worthy charities I support.

THE VOICE OF OY!

American comedy icon Carl Reiner is the first Voice of OY!

Reiner has never been shy about sharing his misfortunes with the world and since OY! integral to his vocabulary, his is the perfect voice for the OY! app. So, every time you send an OY!, CarlReiner says it for you.

But it doesn't stop with Carl Reiner! We will be regularly adding more voices of OY! to the App, so, stay tuned.

●●●○○ BELL
4:21PM
100%
OY!
Login With Facebook
What Is OY!
© Copyright 2014 OY! Inc. All Rights Reserved.

Carl & Mom, Bessie Mathias Reiner

Because Bessie Mathias' Story Deserves to Be Told

CHAPTER THIRTY-FOUR

Because Bessie Mathias' Story Deserves to Be Told

Why did I start this chapter heading with the word 'Because' when I know full well that I am breaking a rule of grammar?

Because three days ago my publisher told me that his girl friend Melissa had read my manuscript and noted that I wrote very little about my mother. Those words made me look at a small cabinet that sits at the bottom of a bookshelf beside my desk. I reached over, swung open the cabinet door and extracted from it an artifact I had inherited from my mother- a New York City School diploma. After much squinting, this almost undecipherable parchment document, besides speaking volumes about my mother's formative years also jogged a memory of some stories I had heard of my mother's infancy-- horror stories about what might have befallen my mother had her parents not fled Romania.

My mother's early life was, by all accounts, a harrowing one. It started with her crossing the Atlantic Ocean as a one year old, the youngest of seven siblings and cared for by a weary, five foot mother and a worrying father. The Mathias family had left Romania to search for peace and prosperity in the United States of America.

I was told that only weeks before her father decided to book passage to the States, he had hidden his year old daughter inside an unused wood burning stove to keep her safe from thrill seeking Cossacks. These marauding men found it great sport to gallop through a village, snatch up a Jewish infant by its ankles and smash its little head into a tree trunk.

Half way across the Atlantic, infant Bessie caught a cold and started running a fever. Living in the bowels of the ship, in dank, dark quarters, eating inedible good and having limited or no toilet facilities, it was almost impossible not to become ill.

At this point, Bessie's father and mother had to deal with the most difficult decision any parent would ever have to make. The Immigration officers in New York Harbor were instructed to refuse entry to all sick passengers and to send them and their entire family back from whence they came. All immigrants were aware of this edict and some parents who had other children besides their ailing child, had to decide whether, for the good of their healthy offspring, they would sacrifice the ailing one. Many tortured parents have lived with the painful memory of the untenable decision they had once been forced to make.

Luckily for my mother, my brother Charlie and me, midway in the crossing, infant Bessie recovered from her cold, which allowed my grandparents, Simon and Caroline Mathias and their nine children, to emigrate to the promised land.

I wish now to make you privy to what is written, but barely legible, on the diploma pictured on the opposing page:

EVENING SCHOOL NO. 13

This Certificate is granted to Bessie Mathias

For faithfulness and proficiency as a pupil

Mary L. Gordon, Principal   Egerton L. Winthrop Jr., President

New York, April 1, 1909

William H. Maxwell, City Superintendent of Schools

Louis Haupt, Chairman, Committee on Special Schools.

This document, whose existence I had almost forgotten, has opened up a pandoras box of information about who my mother was and how she got to be the person I almost knew.

BOARD OF EDUCATION
OF THE
CITY OF NEW YORK.
BOROUGH OF MANHATTAN.

Evening School No. 13

This Certificate is awarded to Bessie Matthias

for faithfulness and proficiency as a pupil.

Mary L. Gordon *Principal.* Egerton L. Winthrop Jr. *President.*

NEW YORK April 1st 1909. William H. Maxwell, *City Superintendent of Schools.*

Louis Haupt, M.D. *Chairman, Committee on Special Schools.*

The first big clue that hit me was the hand written date on my mother's diploma, April 1st, 1901 I knew that my father was born January 1st, 1886, but that was the first time I had ever known of or heard of April 1st, 1901. I was told that my mother's birth certificate had been lost, and since she did not know when she was born, her birthday was never celebrated. Every year when we were teenagers, my brother and I celebrated my father's by gifting him with a box of cigars–Leroy Cigars–five in a cardboard box for twenty-five cents.

For my mother, my brother and I would chip in and buy flowers for her on Mother's Day.

The fact that my mother had received a school diploma in1909 when she was about eight years old, made no sense until I realized that the school from which she graduated was a Kindergarten– a night school Kindergarten! What unconscionable men who afixed their curley-cue signatures to such a dubious document. These monsters condemned my mother to a night school, a night Kindergarten, to free her for her day job in a sweat shop.

Many times I had heard my mother tell of her working as a "Finisher" in a factory that manufactured American flags. As a Finisher, my eight-year-old mother used a small sharp scissors to snip hanging threads from flags that foot-treadled sewing machine operators had just sewn.

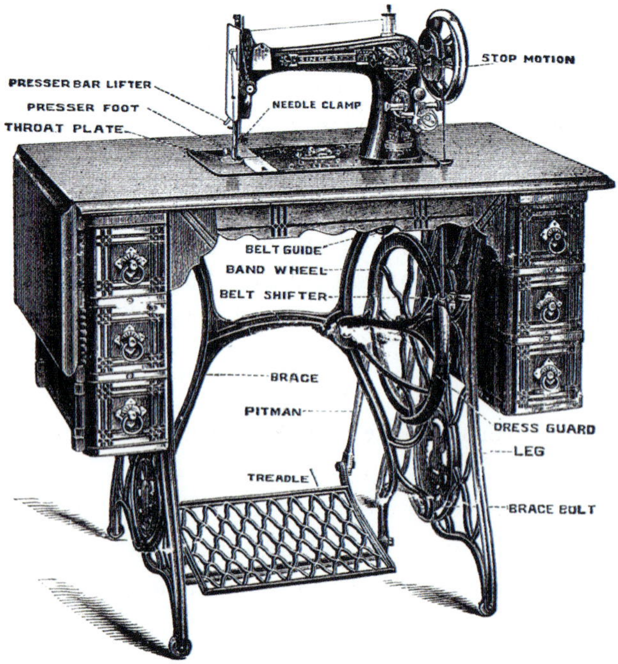

In place at that time, were child labor laws that forbade the hiring of underage workers. These laws were continually broken by factory owners like the ones whot employed my mother. When word got out that a representative from the watchdog, Geary Society, was in the building looking for lawbreakers, my mother was ordered to jump into large empty canvas bin and lie still while heaps and heaps of newly sewed flags were piled on top of her. My mother told of being warned by the factory foreman "not to move a muscle or make a sound until I say its okay." With pounds and pounds of flags all but smothering her, my mother remembered how very difficult it was to breathe and to lie still for sometimes as long as an hour before hearing a muffled, "Okay," from the foreman as he freed her from the weight of the flags.

The Kindergarten Diploma cleared up another mystery, the difference in my parents' ages. We had known that my father was a bachelor until he was thirty and was about ten years older than my mother but now, by computing my mother's date of birth, 1901 with my brother's 1918 and mine 1922, I learned that my mother was just seventeen when Charlie was born and twenty when I saw the light of day. I know now why discussions of my mother's age was off limits. Undoubtedly my father was embarrassed to admit that he had married a teenager.

My parents, for the greater part of their marriage, were completely in sync. My father always praised my mother's ability to handle the family's finances. He relied on her to run the house which was a three room Bronx apartment, in which my father had set up his watch repair bench, at the window in our living room.

As I have outlined, my mother's education ended after kindergarten but she managed so well in the outside world that my brother and I had no idea that she was illiterate. When there was something in the paper that we thought she would enjoy knowing we would hand it to her and she would invariably say, "I don't have my glasses, read it to me," and we did.

When we learned of her inability to read we never discussed it with her or with my father.

In 1953 I had sent a copy of my first novel "Enter Laughing" to my parents and a week or so later my mother called to tell me that she enjoyed the book very much and quickly explained, "Papa read it to me last night –it's very good!"

I thanked her and she added, "But you sent us the wrong book."

I had no idea what she was talking about and I asked why it was "the wrong book" and she said. "By mistake you sent us Estelle's book."

For a moment I did not know what my Mom meant, then realized that when she heard my father read the book's dedication 'To Estelle,' she thought it was my wife's copy.

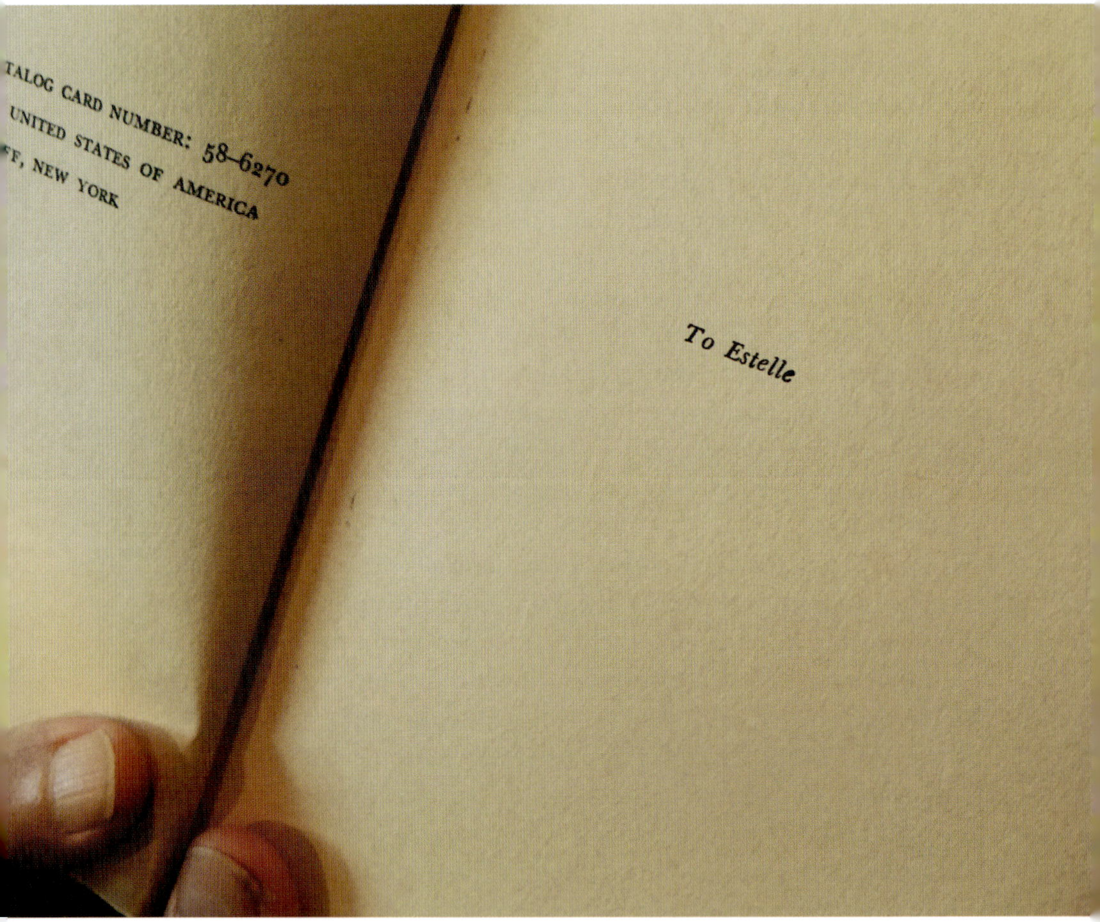

No son ever had a mother who was as big a supporter of his work as mine. She always told me after seeing me perform, "You were the best one!"

She appropriated that mantra when I was in the third grade and she saw me perform in "Six Who Pass While the Lentils Boil." She was sitting next to Mr. Scoppa, the school principal, when told her, "That boy of yours is the best one in the play!"

Decades later after watching me perform on any television show my Mom would declare that I was "the best one!" She told me this even when I worked with Sid Caesar on "Your Show Of Shows." The only negative thing she ever said was, "They they don't give you enough to do."

Nothing gave her more pleasure than when I sent her clippings from newspapers that reviewed my TV performances. She would keep a stack of them in her handbag and show them to her friends. While seated on a bench in Bronx's Crotona Park, she would have one of the women read those reviews aloud. She would then report to me how much they all admired "my acting."

After my mother passed, I always felt sad whenever something positive was written about me, because I had no one to send them to.

Through the years people have told me, "You take after your mother," and I could see it. I had inherited her coloring, her plump-ish lips and her performance genes. To compensate for her inability to read, my Mom was gifted with an extraordinary memory. After seeing a movie, she could tell you the entire story, scene by scene and even recite some of its dialogue. She had a lively, outgoing personality which she successfully used as a matchmaker. Her early beginnings, however, informed her less cheery side, the one that saw disaster lurking at every corner for my brother and me. Her patented phrase was, "The graveyards are full of children who..." and here she would insert,

"...build fires in an empty lot!"

"...fill up on candy before dinner!"

"...didn't look both ways when they crossed the street!"

"...didn't listen to their parents!"

"...played with ruffians and no goodnicks."

"...who don't wash their hands before they eat."

"...who steal and lie!"

One of my Mom's brothers Harry, was a gifted vaudevillian who during the first World War was a member of Irving Berlin's army show, Yip, YiP Yaphank, which featured,"Oh How I Hate to Get Up in the Morning, a song that sold a million copies of sheet music.

In the show, my Uncle sang a solo, "Heart of My Heart" and he played the spoons. He would hold two soup sized spoons back to back, one spoon between his thumb and forefinger and the other between his forefinger and ring finger and he would clack them together in rhythm. I loved when my Uncle Harry would come to our house for dinner and after desert he would give a spoon playing concert. Sadly there are no longer any virtuosos in the field. Spoon playing is today a lost art.

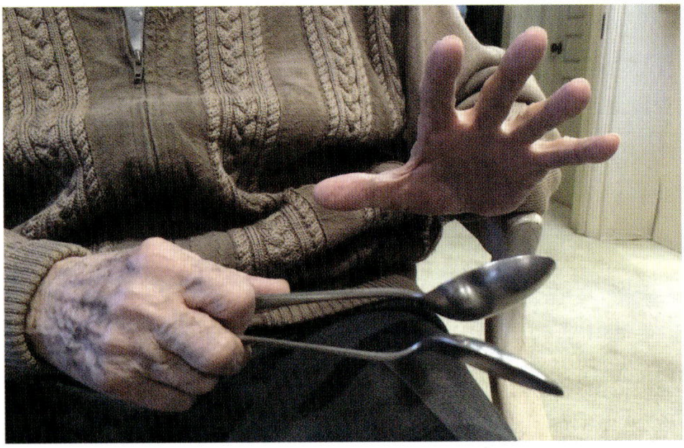

Me impersonating my Uncle Harry

My mother had six siblings, four brothers and two sisters and she liked them all, but her favorite and mine was Uncle Harry.

Mom was so excited each time I won an Emmy, and another opportunity to passing around newspaper clippings. One thing I will forever regret was not offering to let my Mom and Pop have one of my twelve Emmys. I was anxious to keep them all together so someday I could bequeath four of these statuettes to each of my three children.

While on the set of the Dick Van Dyke show, my Pa called from New York to tell me that my mother had passed away. From what I had since learned from her Kindergarten diploma, I realized, sadly, that she was only sixty-one years old. At her funeral my father commented, " I have lost my best friend."

On my piano sits a photo of my Mom as a young girl and what often pops into my mind when I glance at it, was a phrase her brothers and sisters used to describe her... "The Princess!"

Bessie Mathias, 1917

CHAPTER THIRTY-FIVE

Two Examples of Alliterations for Literate People

First Alliteration

Supplied Specially Stylized Sculpted Slippery Soap Slivers Saved For Shaving, Showering & Simply Showcasing

Second Alliteration

Fortuitously Finally Finished Financing Forging Funds For Four Factories to Fulfill orders For Famous, Fake, Fluffy Flowers For their Fifty-Five Fortunate Friends & Feckless, Foolhardy Farmers.

or as most author's say...

The End.

More Books & eBooks by Carl Reiner
Available on Amazon & iTunes:

All Kinds of Love

Continue Laughing

How Paul Robeson Saved My Life And
Other Mostly Happy Stories

My Anecdotal Life

NNNNN

Just Desserts: A Novellelah

I Remember Me

I Just Remembered

The Secret Treasure of Kahka Paka

My heartfelt thanks to my publishers @RandomContent, Lawrence O'Flahavan and Aaron Davis who's talent and dedication helped me shape the look of this book.